Wind on the Heath

Books by George H. Morrison

Highways of the Heart

Wind on the Heath

Wind on the Heath

George H. Morrison

Grand Rapids, MI 49501

Wind on the Heath by George H. Morrison.

Copyright © 1994 by Kregel Publications.

Published in 1994 by Kregel Publications, a division of Kregel, Inc., P.O. Box 2607, Grand Rapids, MI 49501. Kregel Publications provides trusted, biblical publications for Christian growth and service. Your comments and suggestions are valued.

All rights reserved. No part of this book may be reproduced, stored in a retrieval system, or transmitted in any form or by any means—electronic, mechanical, photocopy, recording, or otherwise—without written permission of the publisher, except for brief quotations in printed reviews.

Cover Photograph: POSITIVE IMAGES, Patricia Sgrignoli
Cover and Book Design: Alan G. Hartman

Library of Congress Cataloging-in-Publication Data
   [Afterglow of God]
   Morrison, George H. (George Herbert), 1866-1928.
   Wind on the heath: sermons that breathe the breath of the Holy Spirit / George H. Morrison.
      p.   cm. (The Morrison Classic Sermon Series)
   Originally published: The afterglow of God: London: Hodder and Stoughton, 1912.
     1. Sermons, English—Scotland. 2. United Free Church of Scotland—Sermons. 3. Presbyterian Church—Scotland—Sermons. I. Title. II. Series: Morrison, George H. (George Herbert). The Morrison Classic Sermon Series.
BX9178.M6A47   1993   252'.052—dc20   93-37826
                                                                                 CIP

ISBN 0-8254-3289-8 (paperback)

       1 2 3 4 5 Printing / Year 98 97 96 95 94

Printed in the United States of America

Contents

Publisher's Foreword 7
Introduction 11
Biographical Sketch 13
Dedication Letter 16

1. Unconscious Ministries (Acts 16:25) 17
2. The Lonely People of the Gospels (Ps. 73:26) 23
3. The Omniscience of Love (1 John 3:20) 29
4. Forbidden Battlements (Jer. 5:10) 34
5. Beginning to Sink (Matt. 14:30) 40
6. The Renascence of Wonder (Ps. 109:18) 46
7. The Blindness of Vision (Acts 9:8) 52
8. The Jealousy of God (Ex. 20:5) 57
9. The Contentment of Love (Prov. 15:17) 63
10. The Grace of Continuance (Acts 12:16) 69
11. The Young Man with the Measuring Line (Zech. 2:1–2) ...74
12. The Message of the Colt—A Palm Sunday Sermon
    (Matt. 21:5) 79
13. Angelic Ministry (Heb. 12:22, 24) 85
14. The Attraction of Agnosticism (Acts 17:23) 91
15. The Crowning Vision (1 John 3:2) 98

16.	Christ and the Home—A Christmas Meditation (1 John 4:14) 103
17.	The Responsibility of Hearing (Mark 4:24) 109
18.	The Ministry of Silence (Ps. 46:10) 115
19.	The Comfort of the Universal Presence (Ps. 139:8) 120
20.	The Tears of Jesus (John 11:35; Luke 19:41) 125
21.	On Taking Things Up Again (Neh. 4:15) 130
22.	The Silver on the Idol (Deut. 7:25) 136
23.	Humility Interpreted by Christ (Matt. 11:29) 141
24.	The Smoke in the Temple (Isa. 6:1, 4) 147
25.	The Higher Ministries of Sleep (Song of Sol. 5:2) 152
26.	The Sabbath Day's Journey (Acts 1:12) 158
27.	Patience (Heb. 10:36) 164
28.	Unexpected Issues (2 Chron. 32:1) 169
29.	The Ministry of the Sea (Ps. 95:5) 175
30.	The Second Vision (Zech. 1:18) 181
	Scripture Index 187

Publisher's Foreword

One wonders if the old wit's comment on sermons applies to sermon books as well when he said that a sermon was something a preacher would travel across the country to give but most people wouldn't walk across the street to hear. The initial response to a book of sermons by a turn-of-the-century Scotsman may be somewhat skeptical—in an era dominated by sophisticated media, savvy marketing analysis, and seeker-sensitive communication models, the pressured pastor might wonder about the benefits of reading "relic" sermons.

It was C.S. Lewis who referred to the historical fallacy of regarding works of the past, particularly the classics and the Bible, as irrelevant and untrustworthy based on the criterion of age alone. His comment—"This mistaken preference for the modern books and this shyness of the old ones is nowhere more rampant than in theology."—applies equally as well to pastoral theology.[1]

Issues of truth ought not to be subject to a statute of limitations, but to paraphrase Thomas Oden, we blithely assume that in preaching—"just as in corn poppers, electric toothbrushes, and automobile

---

1. C.S. Lewis, "On the Reading of Old Books" in *God in the Dock,* ed. Walter Hooper (Grand Rapids: Eerdmans, 1970), 200.

exhaust systems—new is good, newer is better, and newest is best."[2] Morrison's sermons represent, without question, not only a different culture (early twentieth-century Scotland which had more in common with the nineteenth century than with our own era) but also a different pastoral model. If pastors are physicians of the soul, then Morrison's ministry had more in common with the hometown doctor who made housecalls (Morrison was legendary for his visitation ministry, sometimes averaging 1000 calls a year) than the modern medical specialist (and pastor) with his sophisticated array of technology.

Morrison's value, therefore, for the modern pastor-preacher does not lie in his insights into church management, church growth, or contemporary worship. Morrison most likely would have eschewed the whole notion of a "contemporary gospel." What he would have championed today—passionately and patiently—was the relevant and compelling presentation of biblical truth that touches both the intellects and the emotions of contemporary listeners. His value for the modern reader lies in appreciating and learning from a style and sermonic approach that was contemporary in its time and whose principles have enduring value.

What can we learn, then, from Morrison? For one thing, he respected the intelligence of his listeners. His sermons are filled with allusions and quotations from a wide range of literature common to the experience of his people—Burns, Milton, Dickens, and Shakespeare—but without any hint of intellectualism or pedantry. Morrison perfectly prefigures Charles Swindoll's comment that preachers should get a good education and then get over it!

Modern preachers would do well to analyze Morrison's style of literary reference and determine the common cultural mediums of our own day. Lacking a similarly cohesive cultural identity, we may have to search harder for the insightful reference or provide a window for the congregation through which to view another world (consider, for example, the difference between quoting Shakespeare and any current TV commercial). Morrison not only spoke of beautiful truths, but he sought to speak the truth beautifully and for help turned to the great English writers and poets.

---

2. Thomas Oden, "On Not Whoring After the Spirit of the Age," in *No God But God*, ed. Os Guinness and John Seel (Chicago: Moody Press, 1992), 195.

Publisher's Foreword

Morrison also placed the sermon in a strategic context—the awful carnage of World War I (where Morrison's own son was killed), the emerging discoveries of modern science, or the urbanization of the once predominately rural Scottish society and the corresponding problems of secularization, alienation, and loneliness. Morrison addressed the developing cultural, social, and political dynamics of the day with both challenging and comforting truths from the Word. If we look closely at the changing demographics and family structures in our own society, we will find ample opportunities for strategically-formulated points of reference.

One other obvious characteristic of Morrison's sermons are their personal appeal. Morrison spoke directly to the needs and concerns of real people: the grieving, the lonely, the guilt-ridden, the worried, and the spiritually hungry. He described his approach as, "It has been my habit. . . at the evening service to allow myself a wider scope. . . to win the attention, in honorable ways, of some at least of that vast class of people who today sit so lightly to the church." Judging from the full pews at the Wellington United Free Church, the success of his sermons can be measured by the phrase used in Mark 12:37—"The common people heard him gladly."

In this new edition of Morrison's sermons, Kregel Publications has attempted to "open a window" into the culture of Morrison's ministry and times. Uncommon terms (in today's usage) have been noted, and the frequent quotes, allusions, and personalities identified. In a few places grammatical constructions that might have rolled off the Scottish tongue have been modified with the modern reader in mind. It is our hope that by appreciating the richness of Morrison's style, readers will be encouraged to creatively speak to both the intellect and emotion of today's congregations. Lewis's comments are a fitting encouragement: "Every age has its own outlook. It is especially good at seeing certain truths and specially liable to make certain mistakes. We all, therefore, need the books that will correct the characteristic mistakes of our own period. And that means old books."[3]

DENNIS R. HILLMAN, SENIOR EDITOR

---

3. Lewis, 202.

Introduction

Dr. George Herbert Morrison has a gift of saying things that we all would have said, had it occurred to us to say them; and he said those inevitable things as we could not, in English prose that had the effect of "poetry on the heart." This quotation of James Denney aptly sums up the "secret"—if there was such a thing—of Dr. Morrison's classic sermons delivered from his pulpit in Wellington Church, Glasgow, Scotland, from 1902 to 1928.

Throughout his ministry he was known for his concentrated study, his regular pastoral visitation, and his constant writing for publication. His appeal lay not in any physical stature, for he lacked that; not in any tricks or oratory, for he never preached for effect; but in the quiet winsome way in which he spoke to the heart from a heart suffused with the love and grace of Christ. He never lost sight of the fact that as a minister of Christ his first concern must be how best to bring his hearers closer to the heart of the Lord.

Although some fifty years old now, his sermons are modern in touch and spirit; the tone and temper are admirably effective for use today. Their simplicity of phrase came out of arduous toil as the writer worked in his preparation. The style is the man—quiet and genial—and his preaching was like this. Morrison was always the pastor preacher, ever seeking to meet life's needs with some word from God.

Whatever he did had the hallmark of preparation and finality. Some sermons came easily like the bird on the wing; others came after much hard work and sweat of mind and heart. The fact that he brooded over his texts with something of an artist's unconsciousness and superb leisure is one of the elements in his power as a preacher. He brooded over the Word of God until it became translucent. His loyalty to Christ and his devotion in the secret place are wedded to his daily practice of study and writing.

His counsel to the young preacher is most revealing as the secret of his own success: "I can think of nothing, except that young preachers will do well to guard against the tendency to rush which is the bane of modern life. The habit of unprofitable bustle and rush, the present-day preoccupation with small affairs and engagements, is withholding many good things from us. For myself it is essential that I have leisure to brood and meditate."

To read and study these selections from the author's many volumes of messages will be to open new vistas of truth and to learn how old and familiar truths can be clothed in fresh and living words which will glow with unsuspected meaning.

RALPH G. TURNBULL

Biographical Sketch

It used to be said that just as visitors to London in bygone days felt that they must of necessity hear Spurgeon or Parker or Liddon, so visitors to Glasgow in more recent years had the feeling that they could not miss hearing Dr. George H. Morrison in Wellington Church. One of the most noted of English Bishops, after fulfilling an afternoon engagement at the University, hurried off to be in time for the evening service at Wellington. And the miner from Fifeshire or the crofter[1] from the Hebrides, spending a Sunday in Glasgow, would have considered the day incomplete if he did not hear Dr. Morrison.

To Glasgow Dr. Morrison's ministry at Wellington was something like what Dr. Alexander Whyte's ministry at St. George's was to Edinburgh. Different in many ways, they were alike in the extent to which they captured the community and maintained their unbroken hold year after year.

Dr. Morrison was a great preacher who was also a great pastor. Of this rather unusual combination he was, indeed, the supreme example.

His genius as a preacher was never more clearly shown than by his

---
1. a tenant farmer

success in solving the problem of the second service. Shortly after his settlement in Glasgow, the afternoon service was giving place to an evening one, but the results in general were not too satisfactory. When Wellington decided on an evening service Dr. Morrison was determined to give it a distinctive character. In the mornings he adhered to the old Scottish tradition of expository preaching.

In the evenings he allowed himself a wider scope, presenting the Christian essentials in a somewhat different setting, and, as he said, calling to his help every type of illustrative aid that appealed to him. He strove to give these evening addresses a strong human interest, in order, as he put it, "to win the attention, in honorable ways, of some at least of the vast class of people who sit very loosely to the Church. The touch is naturally far lighter than in the morning, but this does not mean lack of preparation. I prepare as carefully for the one as for the other." His one aim in preaching, he once said, was "to help people along the road." Here I may interpolate how Dr. Morrison once told me that, after he had fully prepared his subject, he set himself the task of striving to see how simply he could present it. His simplicity, therefore, was not the easy, facile thing some may have supposed it to be; it was the fruit of definite and earnest effort.

The response at his evening service was immediate and striking. The church became crowded to overflowing, long queues formed in University Avenue before the doors were opened and this was no mere passing phase. The same state of matters continued for over twenty-six years, right to the end of his ministry. And he got the class of people he set out to reach. These crowded evening congregations at Wellington made an interesting study in themselves. All classes and all ages were represented, but young men and women were always largely in evidence. Nor were they there because of the prospect of any novelty or sensation. They could only have been drawn because they felt that their wistful longings and inarticulate yearnings were somehow met and answered by the man in the pulpit with the soft voice, the quiet effortless style, and the subtle elusive charm.

There was no clangorous or challenging presentation of a new Evangel. Dr. Morrison's secret was in taking old familiar truths and clothing them in fresh robes of language which made them sparkle with a luster of their own and revealed meanings hitherto hidden and unsuspected. He had a perfect flair in the selection of texts often fresh and suggestive. "He gave them drink out of the

Biographical Sketch 15

depths," "In the day that thou stoodest on the other side," "The deep that croucheth beneath," "Thou didst cleave the earth with rivers," are some that may be quoted, almost at random.

Many of his sermons were prose poems; all of them were suffused with a tender charm and rich in spiritual helpfulness. Volume after volume was published, and G. H. Morrison's sermons found a place in manse libraries everywhere, almost like those of F. W. Robertson of Brighton, while they also very markedly appealed to a wide circle of lay readers. They revealed him to be both a mystic and a man of letters and were acknowledged to place him in the foremost ranks of British preachers. . . .

There are many people who still remember this or that sermon of Dr. Morrison's; there are as many who love to recall instances of his pastoral devotion. His routine visitation, so extensive and incessant, was but one feature of his pastoral activity. Many tales could be told of his constant solicitous care of the sick and those in sorrow or trouble. And no success or joy that came to any member of any family in his congregation was overlooked or allowed to pass without letters or postcards from him, which are still prized possessions.

The end of this notable ministry came swiftly and unexpectedly when Dr. Morrison was at the age of sixty-two and while there was no sign of any waning of his powers and no abatement of his popularity. In the first week of October, 1928, he was back from his summer holiday—he held that a good holiday was a *sine qua non*[2] for a minister—and he was getting into the full stream of another winter's activities. On the Wednesday afternoon he had spent three continuous hours in the homes of his people, and in the evening he gave a memorable address to a small company of workers in the hall of Gorbals Church. On Thursday evening he became seriously ill, and on Sunday morning shortly after midnight he passed away almost before his illness had become generally known.

On the day before he died, when there was a slight rally, he was able to have in his hands one of the early copies of a book to which he had been looking forward—his biography, which I had written at the request of London publishers, and in the preparation

---

2. something essential

of which he had given me every facility with his characteristic kindness.

Although Dr. Morrison did not reach the allotted span, he, if any man, had done what he used to call "a good day's darg."[3] He warned young preachers against unprofitable bustle and rush and preoccupation with small affairs and trifling engagements. A master of method, he so ordered his time that, while he was never idle, he was never hurried or flurried. There was always about him a calm serenity, and as he moved among men he seemed a living epistle of what he preached.

Reprinted from Alexander Gammie, *Preachers I Have Heard*, Pickering & Inglis, Ltd. (London, n.d.)

Dedication Letter

To Fred Turner, Esq., Organist, Wellington Church.

Dear Mr. Turner,

I should like to inscribe this volume to you in token of our happy comradeship in service now extending over many years. You have often been good enough to tell me that you have been helped along the way by the message from the pulpit. I can as truly say that my ministry would have been vastly different without the aid of our service of praise, which you have always led and interpreted with such skill, and reverence, and beauty. That you may long be spared, rich in the esteem of all who know you, to carry on your labor of love is the sincere wish of

Yours most truly,

G. H. Morrison
Glasgow, 1915

---

3. a good day's work

"And the prisoners heard them"
(Acts 16:25).

1
Unconscious Ministries

Strangers in a strange city, Paul and Silas had very violent treatment. They were seized and, without semblance of a trial, were thrust into the inner prison. It was a gloomy and miserable place and might have appalled the spirits of the bravest. Men had been known in that dark cell to curse, and some in black despair to kill themselves. But never, since these walls had been embattled, had any prisoner been known to sing there, and yet at midnight Paul and Silas sang. It was dark, and yet all bright to them. It was exceeding loathsome and yet beautiful.

Stone walls did not a prison make for them, nor iron bars a cage. And so they sang like the lark at heaven's gate—although for them it was a prison-gate—and as they sang, *the prisoners heard them.* Probably some of these prisoners became Christians afterward. It was they who told the story of the Church: told how at dead of night, dull and despairing—hark! the sound of music. And one would recall how it held his hand from suicide, and another how it revived his hope, and another perhaps how it brought back the memory of his mother and his childhood and his home.

Of all that service the men who sang knew nothing. They were totally unconscious of such ministry. They sang because Christ was with them and was cheering them. They sang because they could not help but sing. And all the time, although they never dreamed of it, they were serving others better than they knew, touching old tendernesses, reviving courage, making it easier to suffer and be strong.

Now something of that kind we all are doing. All of us exercise unconscious ministries. When we never dream we are affecting anybody, we are touching and turning others all the time. We fret, and others feel our fretting, though never a syllable has passed our lips. We play the game, and just because *we* play it, folk we have never heard of play it better. We sing at midnight because God is with us and will never leave us nor forsake us, and prisoners in other cells are cheered. One of our writers, a man of genius—yet a man whose moral character was vile—has told us how, when in the grip of shame, somebody took off his hat to him. It was only a custom of familiar courtesy—the instinctive action of a gentleman—yet to him it was a gleam of heaven in his hell.

We never know what we are doing when we do it. Our tiniest actions are touched to finest issues. Like Faithful in the Valley of the Shadow, we lift up our voice because our heart is strong. And some poor Christian, stumbling on behind us on his way also to the Celestial City, thanks God and takes courage at the music. Be quite sure that the very humblest life is full of beneficent unconscious ministries. There is not a note of song we ever raise but the ear of some other prisoner will catch it. Words that we utter and then quite forget—a smile in passing—the clasp of hands in comradeship—have their work in God's strange world to do and will meet us in the rosy-fingered dawn.

This unconscious human helpfulness is one of the chiefest ministries of happiness. Happiness is sometimes selfishness; but happiness is sometimes service. He who resolves at all costs to be happy is generally a very miserable person. In this wide world the things we set our hearts on are so often the things we never get. But when any one is genuinely happy, with a heart at leisure from itself, then happiness is unconscious benediction.

One of the most beautiful poems of Robert Browning[1] is a wonderful thing that he calls *Pippa Passes*. It is a story of murder and of

---

1. English poet, 1812–1889.

guilt, portrayed with the passion and the truth of genius. And then below the house of all this vileness, where vows are treachery and kisses shame, in the exquisite summer morning Pippa passes. She is only an innocent girl, supremely happy, and because she is happy, as she goes she sings. She has no thought of doing good to anybody. She is quite oblivious of listeners. And yet that simple song of girlish happiness, entering the open casement of the house, comes with the very ministry of heaven.

Happiness will sometimes do what bitterest reproach can never do. The man who can sing at midnight because God is with him is doing something for others all the time. To be happy—to be serene and radiant—when the shadows deepen and the cross is heavy, is one of the finest of life's unconscious ministries.

A similar unconscious service is the sweet and tender helpfulness of childhood. Childhood never dreams that it is helping, yet its benedictions are incalculable. A well-known writer has told us that after anxious days he completed a certain book he had in hand. It had cost him much laborious research, and now it was completed. And all the joy of that completed toil, he tells us, was nothing to the gladness he experienced in the pattering footsteps of some little children whom he had taught to love him. Do you remember what they wrote upon the tombstone of a little girl who had gone home? They wrote her name, and then beneath it this—*It was easier to be good while she was with us*. And that is what little ones are always doing in a life that at its best is tortuous—they are making it easier to be good.

How many a man has been true to what is pure through the constraining influence of children. How many a selfish heart has grown considerate when the mystery of motherhood has come. Those eyes of innocence—those pattering feet—those lips that are only still when they are sleeping, have done more to beautify and bless the world than all the legislation of the sages. There is no more real ministry than that, and the wonderful thing is it is unconscious. No child awakens on a summer morning and says, "Today I am going to be a blessing." He is a blessing and he never knows it. He plays in the marketplace and Christ is gladdened. He sings like Paul because he cannot help it—*and the prisoners hear*.

The same unconscious ministry, again, is often a beautiful feature of the sick-room. Patient suffering may be finest service. It is told of

Dr. Norman Macleod, whose memory is still fragrant in our midst, that on one occasion he went to pay a visit to a Sunday School student of his own. He found him stretched upon a sorry pallet, for the lad—an invalid—was dying, amid scenes of crime and destitution. Norman Macleod was not a great divine; Norman Macleod was a great human. Stooping over the bed he said, "My poor lad, I fear you're very weak." "Ay, sir," was the reply, "I'm very weak, *but I'm strong in Him.*" The following Sunday in the Barony Church Dr. Macleod told that story from the pulpit. It was copied into the religious newspapers both here and in America. And by and by, from Scotland and from England and from far-off villages of the United States came testimonies that the story had been blessed. Out in the High Street other lads were serving. Men and women were toiling for the Master. Here in the attic above the crowded vennel[2] was a sufferer who would never serve again. Yet, like Paul and Silas in the dungeon, he sang in his midnight because God was with him, and far away the other prisoners heard. I have heard women lamenting they were useless because they could never leave their little room. Others were out and active in the world; they were nothing but cumberers[3] of the ground. And yet that little chamber was a Bethel, and to enter it was to feel that God was there, and through the streets one walked a better man because of that patient beautiful endurance. Never forget that among life's many ministries the finest may be unconscious ministry. There is an exquisite service of passivity as surely as a service of activity. When the lights are low, when the strong ones bow themselves, when the silver cord is at the point of breaking, you may be serving better than you know.

This, too, is the real value of genuine and unaffected goodness. It is exercising every day a beautiful unconscious ministry. A man may forget all that his mother told him. He will never forget all that his mother *was*. He may lose reckoning of his father's counsel, but never of his father's *character*. It is not the things which we can utter glibly—it is often things we have no power to utter—that fall on other lives with benediction. When Sir Walter Scott[4] was building Abbotsford, he put the bowling green in a peculiar place. And at one corner of it he

---

2. an alley or narrow lane
3. a hindrance, obstacle
4. English novelist and poet, 1771–1832.

built a little summer-house where he might sit of an evening after dinner. And he told Lockhart why he built it there; was it because the view was beautiful? Not so, but that he might sit and listen there to the evening worship of his coachman. Old Peter was a real old Scottish servant. He would not have talked religion for the world. But every nightfall in the year he took *The Book* and "waled a portion wi' judicious care." And then the psalm was raised, and, traveling heavenward to Him who understands our Scottish reticence, Sir Walter heard it, and hearing it was comforted. Old Peter was preaching better than he knew. He was preaching when he never thought to preach. That is what all of us are doing constantly, though we were never in a pulpit in our lives. There are Spurgeons[5] in unlikeliest places—Dr. Parkers[6] in the coachman's cottage—apostles who are cheering all the prison, and they never know that they are doing anything.

Indeed, I believe that much of our Christian service must always be of that unconscious character. When that is lacking, the other is formality. I trust that when this hurrying life is over, you and I shall each have the "Well done." That is the only thing worth living for. It is the only welcome which I want. But I have sometimes thought that if I ever hear it, one of the great surprises of the dawn will be the kind of thing for which it is the reward. Perhaps all these sermons at which I have daily toiled will never be mentioned in that summer morning. And certain ministries of which I knew not anything as I went out and in among you in the shadows here will waken the trumpets on the other side.

Take our soldier lads across in France who are on active service for their king and country.[7] Ask them what they are doing and they will tell you—they are fighting against the tyranny of Germany. Quite so; that is their *conscious* ministry—that is why they responded to the summons—but there is another service not less real. I want to ask, is there any one here tonight who is not better because of those gallant fellows? I want to ask, is there any one in this audience who is not different because of them? Why, sirs, our little sufferings and ailments—our petty crosses—our trifling vexations— we are ashamed to talk of them today when we think of those

---

5. Charles Haddon Spurgeon (1834–92), influential Baptist pastor and preacher.
6. Joseph Parker (1830–1902) English Congregational pastor and preacher.
7. During World War I.

gallant fellows on the field. There they are, nobly enduring all things, and singing how far it is to Tipperary.

It is not exactly a hymn for Christian worship; but, like the wound of Mercutio,[8] it will serve. And though they never dream they have an audience any more than Paul and Silas dreamed it, they sing in their midnight, *and the prisoners hear.* My brother and sister, *that* is unconscious ministry, and we thank God for it and take courage. Men who do their best always do more, though they be haunted by the sense of failure. Be good and true; be patient; be undaunted. Leave your usefulness for God to estimate. He will see to it that you do not live in vain.

---

8. Romeo's friend in Shakespeare's *Romeo and Juliet.*

"My flesh and my heart faileth; but God is the strength of my heart, and my portion for ever" (Ps. 73:26).

2
The Lonely People of the Gospels

Meditating one quiet morning on the men and women of the gospel story, I was led to see, with an unusual clarity, how many of them were lonely people. I had often thought of the heroes of that story and often of the cowards of that story. I knew which characters were gentle there and which were fiery, ardent, or impetuous. But on this particular morning, with unusual clarity, amid the figures that moved across the page, I saw a company of lonely people. With some of them, in very pleasant fellowship, I have been living for the past day or two. Lonely people are almost always interesting—to be lonely is often to be lovable. And so this evening, not taking any text, but casting our eyes over the gospel page, I want to speak of some lonely people there.

Mary—the Loneliness of Love

First, then, I see Mary, and I find in her the loneliness of love. The mother of Jesus was the bride of loneliness. Had her husband Joseph been spared to her through the years, it might have been very different with Mary. She might have turned to *him* when things were difficult, as a woman does to the husband of her heart. But Joseph died when Jesus was a boy, and Mary was left utterly alone, to love, and ponder, and be brokenhearted. Other mothers could compare experiences, but that was what Mary of Nazareth could not do. Even to her family she dare not turn for sympathy, for they thought He was beside Himself. Because Christ was unutterably wonderful, Mary was unutterably lonely, and she was lonely because she loved Him so. Other sons, loving their mothers, would address them in the fond names of endearment. Her son, at the marriage feast, said, "Woman, what have I to do with thee?" (John 2:4). Other sons, with such a peerless mother, would have called her the sweetest mother in the world; but her son, waving His hand across the crowd, said, "Behold my mother and my brothers and my sisters" (Matt. 12:49).

Every mother knows something of that loneliness, as childhood reaches to manhood or to womanhood. There comes a day when the most perfect mother has to make room for others in her daughter's heart. And you have to multiply all that ten thousand fold into the absorbing passion of the Son of God, if you would understand the loneliness of Mary. Not to be able to blast and blight His slanderers when they said He had a devil and was mad—to be utterly powerless to keep Him silent when every word was ringing out His deathknell—and then to stand at the cross and see Him nailed there and hear the exceeding bitter cry He cried—could any loneliness be worse than that? Love is the secret of the sweetest song, and love is the fountain of the deepest loneliness. Sooner or later in this shadowed world a loving mother is a lonely mother. And it is when you remember Mary's love, for a Son who was as mysterious as God, that you come to think of her, in all her glory, as perhaps the loneliest woman in the world.

Thomas—the Loneliness of Doubt

Next there rises before me the disciple Thomas, and I find in Thomas the loneliness of doubt. Thomas is always a solitary figure, as doubters very generally are. You never think of *Peter* as being much alone—he was too ardent and impetuous for that. And you never think of *John* as wooing solitude with his so affectionate and sympathetic heart. But Thomas is always a solitary figure, standing a little apart from cheerful interaction; and he is solitary because he is a doubter. "Let us also go that we may die with him" (John 11:16); he seems to have been "half in love with easeful death."[1] And then on the evening of resurrection Sunday the disciples were gathered—and Thomas was not there. He was a lonely man that resurrection day, perhaps wandering amid the olives of Gethsemane, separated from all glad companionship and separated because he was a doubter. Think of the gladness that filled these eager hearts when they whispered to one another, "Christ is risen." Then think of Thomas, wandering alone, hurrying from all sound of human voices. For him there was no fellowship that evening in the radiant light of resurrection glory; for him there was only the loneliness of doubt.

Here is a woman wedded to a man whom once she pledged herself to love and honor. And she had faith in him, and life was full of sweetness in the quiet and blessed happiness of home. And then there came an hour of revelation when her womanly eyes were opened and she doubted him, and from that hour she has been a lonely woman. That is the very misery of doubt. It is the mother of the hungriest loneliness. Amid the common ties of common life, it makes a solitude and calls it peace. And that is why when any person doubts God and thinks the heaven above the stars is tenantless, sooner or later he or she has a lonely heart. There are those who doubt because they are too lonely; there are more who are lonely just because they doubt. It takes the bond of faith to give us fellowship with child and husband, with comrade, and with Christ. And when faith crumbles and doubt lifts up its head, a man may still be heroic in his duty; but for him, as for Thomas on resurrection evening, there is the anguish of the lonely heart.

The Man by the Pool

Next I see the man by the pool of Bethesda, and I find in him what I call city loneliness. For thirty-eight years he had been crippled—and now he had not a friend in the whole city. There is a loneliness of the moor and of the glen, where there is never a whisper save of the sighing wind. But there is a loneliness which is far worse than that: it is the loneliness of a great and crowded city.

---

1. From "Ode to a Nightingale" by John Keats (1795–1821).

There may be someone here tonight who in our thronging streets is far more lonely than any Highland cottager; and the man by the pool of Bethesda was like that. Round him was all the traffic of Jerusalem, and Jerusalem was a very busy city. The wagons rolled, and children passed to school, and the din of the market fell upon his ear. And at the heart of all that stir and activity, without one single man to give a hand to him, there lay that lonely sufferer by the water. In a country village that scarcely could have happened, for everybody knows everybody in a village. But it can always happen in a teeming city, whether it be Jerusalem or Glasgow. Where life is richest and relationships most varied, and where pleasures flaunt themselves at every corner, it is possible to be more exquisitely lonely than in the solitary shelter of the glen. I had a friend who went to America six years ago, and I shall never forget what he once wrote me. He had spent a year or two in the far west of Canada and then had gone south and settled in the States. And he wrote me that the vast and silent prairie stretching away, endless from his threshold, never so overwhelmed him with a sense of loneliness as did the tumultuous crowding of New York City. Out in the prairie he was for days alone, and yet the strange thing was he was not lonely. There was society where none intruded, and voices calling to him in the wilderness. But in the city where everyone was hurrying, and no one seemed to care a jot for him, he realized he was a lonely man. Spare your compassion for that Highland crofter[2] whose cottage you saw this summer up the glen. There are more lonely people by Bethesda pools than where the burn[3] is lilting through the heather. It may be that passing you tonight out in the lighted streets, and you so happy, there is someone who is heart-weary for a friend.

Judas—the Loneliness of Sin

Then, passing on, I come to Judas, and I find in him the loneliness of sin. Having received the sop at the Last Supper, he went immediately out, and it was night. Why did he hurry from that little company? Nobody drove him from the supper table. Christ did not rise with clenched hands of loathing and hound him on to the

---

2. a tenant farmer
3. a brook or small stream

bosom of the dark. In that brief hour everything is intense, and you see in a flash into the heart of things—into the infinite love of the Redeemer, into the infinite loneliness of sin. We sometimes talk in our foolish way of *social* sins. We might as reasonably talk of gentle murder. There is no such thing in the world as social sin. Sin is the mightiest of anti-social forces. Sin is disruptive in its very nature. It shatters homes and disintegrates companionship. It raises barriers between classes and cleaves society down to its very deeps.

Your little child goes singing through the house and jabbers to you of a hundred trifles. And then some day the child is strangely silent, and shuns you, and forgets his little songs. And then you who are mothers know at once that there is something troubling that little conscience and that the one path to communion is confession. Sin separates the mother from her child. Sin separates the engaged from her beloved. We think that sin is going to make us happy, and in the end it only makes us lonely. From every company, from all society, from love and fellowship, from home and heaven, sin drives a man out into the night. Why did our Lord in that so perfect parable speak of the *one* sheep as going astray? Why not five of them—why not a score of them—where there were a hundred in the flock? It is one of those touches which reveal the Master that from one hundred he separated one, as teaching us the loneliness of sin. One coin, from all the cottage treasury; one sheep, from all the congregated flock; one son, off to a far land, from all the dear companionship of home: so Judas, having received the sop, and the devil having entered into him, went immediately out, and it was night. My younger brother, this is a strange world, and that is invariably the way of it. Every sin you conquer in the battle helps you to a richer comradeship. Every sin you deliberately cling to is a mighty power in you making for loneliness, and to be lonely forever—that is hell.

Jesus—the Loneliness of Grandeur

And so, lastly, I come to Jesus Christ, and I find in Him the loneliness of grandeur. Jesus was supremely lonely, because He was supremely great. There is a type of character with which we are all familiar that makes few demands upon the love of others. It is severe. It aims at self-sufficiency. It will not lean hard on any man. And while we may admire that type of character, and do so justly for it is often noble, we must remember it is not the character of

Christ. It was the passion of Christ's heart that men should trust Him. It was the yearning of His soul that men should love Him. In those rare moments when He was understood, He was thrilled to the finest fiber of His being.

And it is when we think how men misunderstood Him and were blind to all that He was and all He lived for, that we realize the loneliness of Christ. To crave for love and craving not to find it, to have one's every action misinterpreted, to feel that one's dearest do not sympathize, to long for trust and to be met with scorn, for certain natures quivering with life—there is no loneliness which can compare with that, and such was the loneliness of the Redeemer. I do not imagine that had you seen the Christ you would have said, "There goes a lonely man." The Pharisees never thought to call Him lonely. They called Him the friend of publicans and sinners. But the ecstasy of joy that filled His soul when one understood Him and cried, "Thou art the Christ," betrays how unutterably lonely He had been. To be great is to be misunderstood, says Emerson.[4] Was ever man misunderstood like this man? *Eloi, Eloi, lama sabachthani*—and they thought He was calling for Elias. It is only when you remember that, and all akin to it in the evangel, that you come to feel how awful and unceasing must have been the loneliness of Christ.

---

4. From "Spiritual Laws" by Ralph Waldo Emerson (1803–1882).

"For if our heart condemn us, God is greater than our heart, and knoweth all things" (1 John 3:20).

3
The Omniscience of Love

There are some texts of Scripture, and this is one of them, which are very generally misinterpreted. This does not speak of a condemning God, but of a God whose name and character are love. As commonly and perhaps naturally understood, the whole verse has to do with condemnation. We rise from the condemnation of ourselves to the far severer scrutiny of God. If our own imperfect consciences condemn us, how much more awful must the condemnation be of One who is greater than our heart and knows all things. Now if the verse stood in any other context, that would be quite a reasonable rendering. We know that the heavens are not clean before Him, and that He charges even His angels with folly. But let anyone meditate upon the context here and note what the apostle has in view, and he will see that such a rendering is impossible. The apostle is not writing to *condemn*. The apostle is writing to *encourage*. He wants to give the believer, in his despondent hours, something that will encourage and assure him. And so he says, if our own hearts condemn us, there is still one thing that we can do; we can fall back on the omniscience of Love. There are hours when our heart condemns us *not*, says

John, and then we have confidence toward God. We do not doubt Him then—we know we are His children—we have a childlike liberty in prayer. But when the sky is darkened and we lose assurance; when we hear nothing but self-accusing voices, then the only way to peace is to remember that the God of love is greater than our hearts. He knows all the way that we have traveled. He remembers what we have quite forgotten. He is the light and dwells in the light above the spiritual darkness which engirdles us. In those condemning hours when we see nothing except our own exceeding great unworthiness, our Father sees the end from the beginning. That is unquestionably the apostle's meaning, and that unquestionably was the apostle's comfort. From an accusing conscience and a condemning heart he casts us over on an omniscient God. And the unfaltering teaching of this letter is just that that omniscient God is *love*, who, knowing everything, will pardon everything in the infinite sacrifice of Christ.

It has been thought by many, and I believe with truth, that there is a beautiful reminiscence here—a reminiscence of that scene beside the Sea of Galilee in the dear dead days beyond recall. "Simon, son of Jonas, lovest thou me?" "Yea, Lord, *thou knowest* that I love thee" (John 21:15–17). Three times over Simon had denied; three times over was the question put. Who can doubt that on that summer morning, faced by the Lord whom he had treated so, Simon Peter had a condemning heart? Only a week before the Lord had looked on him, and he had gone out into the night and wept. He had promised to play the hero in the crisis, and he had proved the sorriest of cowards. And now, with all these memories of betrayal crying out to condemn him in his heart—"Simon, son of Jonas, lovest thou me?"

What was there that Simon could appeal to? His word? His word had broken like a straw. His past—when only a few days before he had been false and recreant to the Master? But Peter cast himself in his despairing upon the perfect knowledge of his Lord—"Lord, *thou knowest all things,* thou knowest that I love thee." John was present when these words were uttered, and words like these can never be forgotten. They haunt the memory and deepen in significance and live again when the hour of teaching comes. And I for one believe that that sweet hour was vividly present to the mind of John when he gave the Church the comfort of our text. When our heart condemns us, we are like Simon Peter, and like Peter we have naught to plead.

The Omniscience of Love

But when our heart condemns us we can still turn to God, who is greater than our hearts and knows all things. He knows what no one else could ever know, judging us by our failures and betrayals, that we still love Him and still desire His presence and still want to follow and to serve.

Sometimes these self-condemning seasons come when a man has fallen into shameful sin. He has been walking unguardedly and prayerlessly, when lo, his feet are in the miry clay. Perhaps the most deadly sins in a believer's life are sins for which his heart does *not* condemn him—sins so habitual and so customary that conscience long ago has ceased to warn.

But there are other sins in a believer's life so false to all that he has struggled for, that to commit them is to be self-condemned. In such a season the whole world is darkened. We cast our moral shadow on the universe. In such an hour our hope in Christ is dimmed, and all that we have striven for seems vanity. In such an hour, when our heart condemns us, our only refuge from despair is this, that God is greater than our heart and knows all things. He knows all the past and all the future; He knows that we were meant for better things. He knows that in the heart of the prodigal there is still to be found the memory of home. He knows that the precious blood of Christ is able to cleanse the very vilest stain, and that though our sins be as scarlet they shall be white as snow. All that, when our heart condemns us, we forget. All *that* the God of love never forgets. He knows how weak we are—how we are tempted—He knows our frame and remembers we are dust. Things which are blotted out when we have sinned—the faith and prayer and toil of long ago—He knows and knowing will be merciful and being merciful will lead us home.

Another season of self-condemnation is the silent season of the night. When the eyes are sleepless and the brain is busy, a very common visitor is fearfulness. There is a vivid picture in the Song of Solomon of the terrors which beset an Eastern king. Sixty mighty men stand around his tent because of fear in the night. But one does not need to be an Eastern king, haunted by vision of poison or of dagger, to know the fear that lurks in the darkness. Dim and shadowy and ill-defined anxieties are the worst of all anxieties to bear. Troubles wholly known are bearable; it is when half-known that they sap the heart. And such are the forms that visit us by night when the eye is sleepless and the brain is busy—oppressive shadows, spectral and illusive. In the light of day we see things as they are. We see things in their just proportions then. And perhaps the essential quality of courage is just to see things in their true proportions. But in the nighttime there are no proportions; everything is confused and undefined; we lie at the mercy of vague and spectral terrors. Sometimes that fear in the night regards our health, sometimes our future or our children. Sometimes it overwhelms us in the silence with an utter hopeless sense of our unworthiness. And it is in such seasons, when our heart condemns us, that from the verdict of our heart, we should appeal to Him who is greater than our heart and knows all things. It is the duty of every believer to abstain from judging in an hour of gloom. The verdict of a desponding hour is the most worthless verdict in the world. Only He who dwells within the light can see things as they are and as they shall be, and He is greater than our heart and knows all things. He . . . knows all that tomorrow shall bring forth, knows all that we shall need tomorrow. He . . . knows our children and how we pray for them. And He who is thus omniscient is Love, and does not will that any should perish. He is the Lord God, merciful and gracious.

Another self-accusing hour in life is the hour when opportunity is over, the hour which is always striking for humanity when the home is empty and the grave is full. Such a season, like all life's greatest seasons, is filled with very diverse feelings. There is the sorrow of parting in it; there is loneliness; there is a strange unreality about familiar things. But always, in such seasons of bereavement, there is the arrowy feeling of remorse, for what was never done or done unkindly, before the pitcher was broken at the fountain. It is *not* when love has been shallow that it hurts. It is when love has been *real* that it hurts. It is when the service of love has never faltered that love feels, when all is over, its unworthiness. It is the mother who has loved her children and laid her life down daily for her children, who feels, when the flowers are fresh upon the grave, what a far better mother she might have been.

There is a remorse which is as black as hell and has no refuge in Almighty God. It is the remorse of cruelty—of base neglect—of shameful desecration of life's sanctities. And yet I question if that satanic misery, falling as it does on hardened hearts, is half so keen or arrowy or exquisite as the remorse of love. The hour of sorrow is an hour of darkness, and in darkness we do not see things as they are. Out of a million words that we have spoken, one word—perhaps a bitter one—remains. Out of a thousand days of quiet happiness, which leave no living memorial in sorrow, one day abides in which the tongue was bitter or in which the deed was unthinking or unkind. Beloved, when our hearts condemn us so, there is just one thing that we can do. When our hearts condemn us we can turn to God, who is greater than our hearts and knows all things. We can appeal to Him. He knows it all. He has been watching through the forgotten years. And there we can leave our cause in quiet confidence, until the day break and the shadows flee away.

In closing, let me point out to you that there is another self-accusing hour in life. It is the hour of spiritual privilege, like that of the holy season of the Lord's Supper. Will you recall that scene upon the Sea of Galilee when the nets were filled until they began to break? Will you recall how Simon Peter cried, "Depart from me, O Lord, I am a sinful man" (Luke 5:8). Faced by the wonderful goodness of the Lord to him, treated with a love that was magnificent, Peter was conscience-stricken and ashamed. I do not know how you may feel, my friend, when people are wonderfully good to you; but I can at least answer for what *I* feel—I feel like an unworthy and undeserving wretch. And if the wonderful goodness of others to us gives us often the self-condemning heart, how much more the goodness of the Lord! That is why, at the table of the Master, conscience so often wakes within the heart. "Here, O my Lord, I see Thee face to face," and seeing Thee face to face my heart condemns me. Beloved, if your heart condemns you, make your appeal to the eternal Father, for He is greater than your heart, and knows all things. He knows that you are not satisfied. He knows that you are hungering and thirsting. He knows that you are poor and needy, and that you have no other refuge. *Sursum corda.*[1] Lift your heart to Him. Cast yourself on His omniscient love. The eternal God is your refuge, and underneath are the everlasting arms.

---

1. From the Anglican order of service, addressed by the celebrant to the congregation before the Preface or prayer of thanksgiving.

"Take away her battlements, for they are not the Lord's" (Jer. 5:10).

4
Forbidden Battlements

That was an exceeding bitter cry to be uttered in the ear of Judah. It must have been a heartbreak to the prophet, that such a message was given him of God. Jerusalem was God's beloved city; in infinite mercy He had tended her. Through fair and foul, for many a weary year, God had upbuilt her into queenly beauty; and now when the sun had vanished from her sky, and the enemy was thundering at her gate, this was the message of God's prophet. Those battlements—they were the city's pride. They were the hope and comfort of the capital. Broad-based—firmset—with tower and bastion—they could defy assault and laugh at the invader. And then, uplifted through the city streets like the wail of a chill wind in winter, came the harsh reiterated cry, "Take away her battlements, for they are not the Lord's." It sounded like a very cruel cry. As a simple matter of fact, it was the opposite. Judah was staying herself upon securities that had no sanction in the will of heaven. And God commanded that they be swept away, not in hatred but in tender mercy that Judah might be brought to lean again upon the strength of the everlasting arm. That was the cry which went ringing through Jerusalem. That cry has gone ringing down the ages. You hear it in individual life and not less audibly

Forbidden Battlements

in national and social life. And what I want to do tonight is this: I want to try to catch the echoes of it.

To begin with, I would think of the Bible, that volume to which our debt is infinite, that revelation of the love of God, crowned in the priceless gift of a Redeemer. It is the book whose words we learn in infancy; it is the book we turn to when we die. It is the book that comforts us in suffering, cheers us in struggles, heartens us in toil. It is the only book that never fails us amid all the change and challenge of the years, for it is higher than our highest thought, and it is deeper than our deepest need. In it we find the language of our prayers; in it the passionate cry of our confession; in it the sins that link us with the beasts; and in it the joys that bind us to the angels. In it we read the story of that sacrifice which is far too good to have been false, without which we cannot live and cannot die.

Go ask the sufferer upon her sickbed. Ask the woman who has proved its promises and clung to them in sunshine and in storm. Ask the sinner who has found a Savior there in the hour when his feet were on the brink of hell and vain was the help of man. It is such things that are the valid proof of God in Scripture. And wherever men have buttressed up the Bible by proofs which were never intended by its Giver, there has come the voice that once was heard in Judah, "Take away her battlements, for they are not the Lord's." That is what true research has always done—all loving, patient, critical inquiry. It has not touched the living Word of God. It has removed the battlements God never built. And so it has drawn us nearer to that heart which is forever throbbing in the Word, in whose mercy is our only hope and in whose will our peace.

The same thing is also true of many of the greatest doctrines of the Bible. Men have sought to fortify and guard them by battlements which the Lord will not acknowledge. I read in Scripture that I am saved by faith. I read that the death of Christ was an atonement. I read that at the dawn of the third day our Savior rose victorious from the dead. I learn that in one God there are three persons, the Father, the Son, and the Holy Spirit; I gather that in our Savior were two natures. Now, of course, I am perfectly aware that we are to give a reason for our faith. If God be God, then He will not insult us by giving us a faith which is irrational. But the things by which we live are mysteries—mysteries to us though not to Him—and you will never prove them by your argument. Give me the testimony of believing hearts, and I have learned that we are saved by faith. Give me the witness of regenerate men, and I have learned that in Christ there is atonement. And it is when men who have never experienced it elaborately build up their bloodless arguments, that I hear the voice which once was heard in Judah, "Take away her battlements, for they are not the Lord's."

I have read treatises on saving faith that have almost turned me to a skeptic. I have read volumes on the atoning death that have handled it like a problem of geology. My Christian friend, if I am not mistaken, these are battlements God never owns for the defending and the aid of His truth. The battlement of God for the atonement is the sinner who can say "Christ died for me." The fortress of heaven for the resurrection is the present action of the living Christ. The walls that guard the truth of saving faith are the sweet and beautiful and lowly lives that have learned to trust and in trusting to be glad in a love that will not let them go.

Or passing from our conception of the Bible, we might turn our thoughts to the story of the Church. For this is the cry of every Reformation, "Take away her battlements, for they are not the Lord's." Our thoughts go back to the medieval Church. What mighty defenses she had raised around her. What buttresses and bulwarks she had built! She seemed impregnable, that medieval Church with her battlements deep as hell and high as heaven against which kings and emperors might fling themselves and fling themselves in vain. Outside her boundaries there was no salvation. It was she and she alone who could give pardon. It was through her that the bliss of heaven was gained. Through her the pain of purgatory was shortened. Her wealth was boundless and her civil power supreme. She could make monarchs and cast them down again. To be her favorite was to be blessed, and to be excommunicated was death. Battlements of pride and place and power—battlements high as heaven and deep as hell—battlements forged and fitted with such intricacy as to defy the batterings of time.

And then, across the streets of Europe passed a heroic and prophetic figure, crying as Jeremiah cried, "Take away her battlements, for they are not the Lord's." The strange thing is that they *were* taken away—such tremendous power is in prophetic voices! Her walls were ruined—her defenses shattered—her pride and glory humbled to the dust. And once again, as long ago in Judah, that voice which seemed so treacherous and ruthless was the voice of the loving-kindness of the Lord. Out of the ruins of an earthly Church arose the form of a Church that was divine. The concubine of Caesar perished and out of her grave arose the bride of Christ. And faith revived, the word of God was read, and the love of Christ became a great reality. Spiritual peace and joy came back again.

My Protestant hearer, we have no part tonight in that ancient woman and her glory but we must see to it that in other ways we are not building unacknowledged battlements. No longer do we grasp at temporal power to fortify the position of the Church. No longer does the Church entrench herself behind the power of the keys or purgatory. But is there not a danger lest our Church should seek to guard and fortify herself by battlements which the Lord will not acknowledge? When we think to prosper by organization instead of by the power of living faith; when the meeting for prayer is miserably empty and the entertainment is crowded to the door; when sacred concerts take the place of worship, and when there is vulgar advertisement of flashy sermons, does not the cry go ringing through the Church, "Take away her battlements, for they are not the Lord's"? Take them away; they are a mockery. They are no fortress for the bride of Christ. Take them away, and give us back again a Church whose battlement is faith in God, a Church whose prayer is uttered from the heart, whose music is the simple voice of praise, and whose preaching to the souls of sinful men is the message of the everlasting gospel.

But not only is that true of churches; it is also true of individuals. It is true, for instance, of those strange reversals which come so often to the prosperous man. Sweet are the uses of adversity; sweet also the uses of prosperity. It is God's reward for faithful honest labor, and being such it is a blessed thing. Yet who has not seen, and seeing sorrowed for, that fatal power inherent in prosperity to deaden character and weaken faith and cast a shadow upon the childlike heart? Houses and parks and pleasances and gardens—troops of friends, servants, and happy children—how often do these rise like battlements between the individual soul and God; and how often in these very things has a man thought to find his strength and safety amid the tears and trials of mortality. Then comes, in some unexpected hour, "the blind fury with the abhorred shears."[1] And gone are the priceless pictures, and the books, and the pleasant lawns, and the deferential service. And what is *that* but the prophetic voice crying across the life as through Jerusalem, "Take away her battlements, for they are not the Lord's"? It is in hours like that persons see again. It is in hours like that they feel their need of heaven. The battlements are gone, but God remains. Their only help and refuge is in Him. And so have many found what Judah found, that the prophetic cry which seemed so ruthless has been the beginning of a blessed peace.

Something, too, of the same kind is seen in the experiences of the moral life. We might think for instance of St. Paul. Filled with the burning passion to be righteous, Paul had striven for holiness magnificently. Longing eagerly for peace with God, he had toiled heroically to be justified. And when his hope was dim and when the fight was fierce, what unassailable battlements he had, behind which there was shelter for his soul! Circumcised the eighth day; of the stock of Israel, of the tribe of Benjamin; concerning zeal, persecuting the Church; touching the righteousness which is in the law, blameless. What towers are here—what mighty walls and bastions—what fortresses of privilege and birth, to guard and shelter the besieged soul! Then came the hour when he met with Christ as he was taking his journey to Damascus. In that great hour he saw his Savior, and in that great hour he saw himself. And once again, right through that life of his, as through the streets of Judah long ago, rang out that old prophetic cry, "Take away his battlements, for they are not the Lord's."

"What things were gain to me," he writes, "these I counted loss for Christ" (Phil. 3:7). All that he trusted in and made his pride was rent and ruined and removed. His circumcision—his unsullied ancestry—his zeal—his strict observance of the law—all were lying tossed and shattered at his feet. Ah yes, but only think of what had happened! He found that hour all that he had been seeking: the inward peace, the reconciliation, and the righteousness which he had sought in vain. All that his battlements could never give him, of safety and security and song, was given to him in the hour he found a Savior.

---

1. From "Lycidas" (1637) by John Milton (1608–1674).

Now that is a story of very long ago, and heaven and earth have passed away since then. But that experience of the great apostle is still repeated in a thousand lives. Not by the privileges of their Jewish ancestry do men now build a refuge for their souls; not by the fact that they were born and bred of the stock of Israel and of the tribe of Benjamin. But none the less in the day of spiritual conflict and in the craving for blessedness and peace, men still have battlements in which they trust. Sometimes it is rite or sacrament, sometimes that they are members of a church, or sometimes that they have lived a virtuous life or are men of honorable reputation. And how often, at this very hour, to those who trust in themselves that they are righteous, there comes the cry which came to the apostle, "Take away her battlements, for they are not the Lord's." It may come in the dark day when sin has conquered. It may come in the solemn hour of dying—that sense that all that we trusted in is vain, and that the walls we built to save us are in ruin. And it is then that we are cast on Christ, our only fortress and defense, who lived to inspire us, who died to save us, and who is all in all to every one who trusts Him. "Nothing in my hand I bring. Simply to Thy cross I cling"[2] It is when all the battlements are ruined that in victorious despair a man says that. And it is only when a man says *that*, and says it because he knows it true, that for him there is peace and happiness and courage and the radiance of sunrise on the hills.

---

2. "Rock of Ages," by Augustus Toplady (1740–78).

"Beginning to sink, Peter cried, Lord, save me" (Matt. 14:30).

5 ✓
Beginning to Sink

There are two sights in human life which fill the heart with profound sorrow. The first is that of a person who has sunk. When we see a face made loathsome by iniquity and think that once it was innocent and childlike; when we hear of somebody who bore an honored name, but is now in the depths of degradation—that is one of life's most piteous spectacles. It arrests even the worldly-minded who cherish no ideals for humanity. How much more must it sadden one who has anything of the vision of Christ Jesus. Men who are sunken—women who are sunken—are the heartbreak of the home and of the city. There is such infinite, pathetic waste in a wasted, miserable life. But to the seeing eye and the perceiving heart there is another spectacle which is not less tragic—it is that of the man who is *beginning to sink*. Beginnings are always mighty and momentous for every eye that has the power to see. Much of our knowledge and our power today springs from our modern study of beginnings. And here in our text tonight we have an instance, not of a man who has sunk into the depths, but of a man who is beginning to sink. Shall we look at him in that light for a little bit?

The first thought to force itself upon me is that *it was Peter's temperament which put him in this danger*. He began to sink not

Beginning to Sink

because he was wicked; he began to sink because he was Simon Peter. The other disciples were all safe and sound. It never occurred to them to leave the vessel. They were men of sagacity and commonsense and knew the difference between land and water. But Peter was reckless, headstrong, and impetuous, acting on the impulse of the moment. Peter followed the dictate of his heart and never waited for his laggard reason. In a sense that was the glory of his character. It made him do what no one else would do. It gave him the charm of daring and enthusiasm of that unexpectedness which always fascinates.

But those very qualities that in the hand of Christ were to go to the upbuilding of the Church sometimes brought him to the verge of ruin. It was only Peter who would begin to walk, and it was only Peter who would begin to sink. He was led into peril on these stormy waters because of what was self-forgetful in him. And it may be there is someone here tonight who has not sunk yet, but is beginning to sink because he has a temperament like that. Our perils do not always reach us through our worst. Our perils sometimes reach us through our best; through what is charming in us, and delightful and self-forgetful and enthusiastic. And so like Peter we begin to do what the cold and calculating would never do, and then like Peter we begin to sink. That is why every man needs to be saved not only from his sin but from his self. That is why God, in His holy love to save us, gave us not a message but a Man. For our brightest social qualities may wreck us. A touch of genius may be our ruin. For all that is implied in that word *temperament*, we need the keeping of the Lord Jesus Christ.

The next thing to arrest me here is that Peter began to sink *in very familiar waters*. I suppose if you had asked him if he knew them, he would have replied that he knew them, every inch. Some of us, who spend our summers by the Clyde,[1] think we are very familiar with the Clyde. And if love be at the source of all true knowledge, then indeed it may be that we know them. But if you want a true and perfect knowledge, it is not to the summer visitor you look, but to the fisherman who was cradled by its shores. Now Simon Peter was a fisherman, and all his life had been spent beside that lake. He had played on its shores as a little child; he had known

---

1. The Clyde River in southern Scotland.

it in summer and in winter. And it was *there,* in these familiar scenes, amid what was habitual and customary, that he began to sink. There was another occasion when he began to sink, and that was in the High Priest's palace at Jerusalem. He was a stranger there—in unfamiliar scenes—among men and women who knew nothing of him. Here it was different. Here he was at home. He was among those who knew him and who loved him; and here he began to sink. It is a very sad and pitiable thing when a man begins to sink away from home, when he goes away into a distant land and forgets the God of his father and his mother. But the peril for you and me tonight is the peril of Peter on the lake of Galilee—that we begin to sink amid familiar waters. Beginning to sink in India is sad, but beginning to sink at home is almost worse—forgetting the sanctuary, the bended knee, purity, temperance and tenderness. And if there is anyone here tonight who is beginning to sink—at home, amid those who love and pray—now is the time to cry as Peter cried, "Lord, save me, or I perish."

Another feature which I note is that Peter began to sink *after loyal discipleship.* He had known Christ and had loved and followed Christ before this hour of peril on the lake. We all remember that great hour in history when Peter had been called to the discipleship. Then he had left all and followed Jesus; he had made the full surrender to the Lord. And from that hour he had companied with Jesus, seen His miracles, heard His words, and enjoyed the infinite blessings of His friendship. No one would doubt the reality of that. That self-surrender was intensely real. And Peter loved his Lord, knew His power, and was never happy except in His companionship. And it was after all that rich experience—that self-surrender and devoted service—that Peter on the lake began to sink. He was no raw and inexperienced youth. He was one who had heard the calling of the Master. He was no beginner in the higher life. He was a man who had done yeoman service.

And the sad thing is that in every community there are men and women who begin to sink, not in their raw and inexperienced youth, but after years of discipleship and service. Sometimes it is the deceitfulness of riches which causes it. Sometimes it is growing absorption in business. Sometimes it is the constant subtle influence of one who is unspiritual in the home. Sometimes it is weariness in well-doing and the dropping of the life to lower levels, from secret

Beginning to Sink

clingings that no one knows but God. No one would say such lives were sunken lives. I am not speaking of moral wrecks and tragedies. I am speaking of men who are still of good repute, still kind at home, still diligent in business. And yet one feels they have begun to sink. They are not the men we remember in the morning. There is a different accent in their speech and a different atmosphere around their character. Do these simple words make anyone uncomfortable? I pray God they may be winged to the conscience. I want to awaken people out of their security, as Peter was wakened on the sea of Galilee. I want them to recall their past discipleship to compare it with what they are tonight, and then to cry, as Simon Peter cried, "Lord, save me, or I perish."

Also to be noted is this fact, that Peter began to sink *on a permitted path*. When he began to sink, he was no trespasser; he was going where Christ permitted him to go. Had our Lord cried to him across the water, You are a madman if you try to come; had He cried to him, You shall not come—on the peril of your life I bid you halt—why then we should have understood it better—we should have said it served him right to sink, for then he would have been disobeying Christ, and the wages of disobedience is death. The point which I want you all to notice is that Simon Peter was not disobeying. Our Lord had not forbidden him to come. Our Lord had rather invited him to come.

And so I learn that on permitted paths—on ways that are sanctioned by the voice of heaven—it is possible now, as on the lake of Galilee, for men and women to begin to sink. There are ways that are forbidden to every child of man. God writes his flaming "No Thoroughfare" upon them. And just for the reason that this is a righteous universe, the person who sets foot on them begins to sink immediately. But the strange thing is that even when God says, "Come," and opens up the way that we may walk in it, even *there* it is always possible to sink. That is true of the blessedness of home. It is true of all social and Christian service. A man may preach the everlasting gospel, yet run the risk of being cast away. And therefore amid all our privileges and all the gifts which God has blessed us with, "Lord, save us, or we perish."

Equally notable is this, too, that Peter began to sink *when he began to fear*. And the Scripture tells when he began to fear: it was when he took his eyes off his Lord. There is not a trace that the wind had grown more fierce while the disciple was walking on the water. It had been just as fierce, and the waves had been just as boisterous when he had sprung from the gunwale of the boat. But then he had thought of nothing but the Master and had eyes for nobody except the Master; so long as that continued he was safe. Looking to Christ he could go anywhere. The very sea was as a pavement to him. Looking away from Christ he was as other men, and the perils that surrounded him were terrible. And then he regretted the rashness of his venture and saw nothing around him but the seething waters, and so Peter began to be afraid and beginning to be afraid, began to sink. That is true of every kind of life. It is true especially of spiritual life. In the perilous calling of the spiritual life. To lose heart is to lose everything. And that is why the Lord is always saying to us, "My son, give me your heart," for only in His keeping is it safe. It is a simple message—looking unto Jesus, and yet it is the message of salvation. To trust in Him and to keep the eye on Him is the one secret of all Christian victory. When we have failed to do so in the stress of life, as all of us, like Simon Peter, fail. Then there is nothing left but to cry with Peter, "Lord, save me, or I perish."

I think, too, we may reasonably infer that *the other disciples knew nothing of all this.* When Peter began to sink, they never noticed it. To begin with, you must remember that all this happened about the time of daybreak. Then the waves were boisterous and in wild confusion, so that the feet of Peter often would be hidden. And if they failed to recognize their Lord when He walked in majesty upon the waters, they were not likely to see Peter clearly. When we see someone on the point of drowning, our first instinct is to cry out. But we have no hint of anyone crying here, save the disciple himself in his distress.

And so I gather from these converging hints that when Peter began to sink into the deeps, no one saw it except himself and Christ. I should not wonder if in this church tonight there are some people just like Simon Peter. They have not sunk yet. They are not degraded; they are just beginning to sink. Yet no one at home knows anything about it. No one suspects it or has ever dreamed of it. No one would believe it for a moment. When a man has sunk, then there is no disguising. The story is written that he who runs may read. There is nothing hidden, but it shall be revealed, whether of things in heaven or things in hell. But when a man is just beginning to sink, it may be utterly different from that; it may be a secret between himself and God. His nearest and dearest may not dream of it; his mother and father may be in total ignorance. He may come to church, engage in Christian service, and take his place at the communion table. We say of him, How well he is getting on—what a fine young fellow he is turning out to be! And all the time, unheard and unobserved, the man is crying, "Lord, save me, or I perish." It ought to make us very tenderhearted. It ought to make us always very prayerful. There are things happening here tonight among us we never suspect, things of which we never dream. For the heart knows its own bitterness, and a stranger does not meddle with it; but there is One who is not a stranger and *He* knows.

And so I close by saying that when Peter began to sink, *his Savior was not far away.* Immediately He put out His hand and grasped him. How far Peter had walked upon the water the narrative of Scripture does not tell us. Shall we say fifty yards, or shall we say a hundred yards?—it matters not whether fifty or a hundred. If the nearest human hand was fifty yards away, the hand of Christ was not fifty yards away; immediately He put forth His hand and helped him. My brother, just beginning to sink, will you remember that Christ is at your side? All human help may seem very far away; remember that *He* is not very far away. He is near you now, near you where you sit. You need Him greatly and He is there for you. Cry out tonight, "Lord, save me, or I perish," and He will do it to the uttermost for you!

"Open thou mine eyes, that I may behold wondrous things out of thy law" (Ps. 109:18).

6
The Renascence of Wonder

There died not long ago in London a gentleman of whom the public knew but little, but who exercised no inconsiderable influence upon the literature of our time. Mr. Watts Dunton[1] was a poet, and as a poet he sought to be remembered. He was a novelist, one of whose novels were very widely read, and are read still. And he had such delicate and loving insight into all that is true and good in literature that Rossetti[2] thought him the first critic of all time. Whether his poems will live or not is questionable, but there is one phrase he coined which certainly will live. It was he who gave us the now familiar phrase *the renascence of wonder*. His death has constrained some of us to meditate again on the rebirth of wonder.

One of the hopeful features of the present day—and we ought to note it amid much that is discouraging—one of the hopeful features of the present day is just that wonder is coming to its own again. Some of us here tonight are old enough to remember a time when it was different. As with Mr. Gradgrind in *Hard Times*,[3] the motto of

---
1. Walter Watts Dunton (1832–1914), English critic and poet.
2. Dante Gabriel Rossetti (1828–32), English poet and painter.
3. By Charles Dickens (1812–70), English novelist.

thirty years ago was, "Never wonder." And it would be a very interesting study, though one scarcely congenial to the pulpit, to trace the causes in science and society of that hard, unwondering, temper. It is enough to say, with profound gratitude, that that temper is disappearing now. Silently—almost imperceptibly—there has come a renascence of the sense of wonder. Men are awakening to the mystery of things, to the reality of the unknowable; to the fact that there are great and vital truths which it is quite beyond our power to prove.

Of course there is a wonder born of ignorance which must inevitably pass away. It is what Crabbe calls in his grim poem "the rustic wonder of the village boy."[4] You show a savage a Geneva watch, and in his eyes it is a miracle. He will call the village in intense excitement to share in the wonder of his ignorance. And naturally, as knowledge widens and the principles of mechanics are explained, such ignorant wondering ceases to exist. But that is only the counterfeit of wonder. True wonder is never expelled by what we know. On the contrary, the more we truly know, the more wonderful does everything appear. In the elementary laws of all mechanics there is more real mystery for thoughtful men than for the savage in that watch which is a miracle.

It was one of my privileges as a student to listen to the lectures of Lord Kelvin.[5] On what these lectures actually taught me—perhaps the less said the better! And yet I and many of my fellow students, looking back upon these golden days, feel how incalculable is our debt to them. Here was a man whose knowledge was profound, who moved with the perfect ease of conscious mastery—a man who spoke, and in every seat of learning the wisest were content to listen. And yet of arrogance was not one trace, of the pride of intellect absolutely nothing, but through everything a certain sense of wonder as in the presence of mysteries unfathomable. That and that alone is genuine wonder—the wonder not of ignorance but of knowledge, the wonder that does not vanish when we know but grows and deepens with everything we know. It was the wonder of the Apostle Paul. It was the wonder in the heart of Jesus. And it is

---

4. From "The Village" by George Crabbe (1755–1832), English poet.
5. William Thompson (Lord) Kelvin (1824–1907), British physicist and mathematician.

the wonder we shall feel forever in the perfected knowledge of eternity.

It is not knowledge, then, which is the foe of wonder; it is something far more commonplace than that. The blight that wilts our faculty of wonder is the familiarity which begets contempt. Someone has said that if all the stars were to cease shining for a hundred years and then were suddenly to flash on again, there is not an eye on earth but would be lifted heavenward and not a heart but would break forth in praise to God. But the stars were there when we were little children, and they will be shining in the heavens tonight. And to us the spectacle is so familiar that we have lost the wonder of it all. "I would rather live in a cottage and wonder at everything," says Ruskin,[6] "than live in Warwick Castle and wonder at nothing." And that is the peril of those who live in Warwick Castle and in a castle more magnificent than Warwick, a castle whose fretted ceiling is the heaven, whose tapestry is the garniture[7] of summer, whose gateways are touched with the glory of the east, and whose loud-resounding organ is the sea. Live for forty years in Warwick Castle, and the wonder of it is scarcely felt at all. Live forty years in such a world as this, and a certain blindness falls upon the eyes. And therefore the need that when the evening falls, the morning breaks, and the summer comes again, we should pray as the psalmist prayed so long ago, "Lord, open thou mine eyes that I may see" (Ps. 119:18).

May I say in passing that all great experiences tend to recreate the sense of wonder? Sickness, sorrow, death, conversion have a way of bringing new wonder into everything. That most winsome of all saints, St. Francis, tells us of a terrible illness which he had. For weeks his life was hanging in the balance, and he only wanted to go home to God. And then he tells us how, when he recovered and went out for the first time on the Italian hills, there was a joy—a wonder—an ecstasy in nature that made the world like a paradise of God. That was in Italy long ages since. Are there none here who have had like experience? None who have known this blessing of a sickbed—that they have felt afresh the wonder of the world? And I suggest that in the will of God, which is as merciful as it is wise,

---

6. John Ruskin (1819–1900), English writer, critic, and social reformer.
7. adornment or decoration

The Renascence of Wonder

that recreating of the sense of wonder may be one purpose of many an hour of discipline.

I remember once at a street corner hearing a man describing his conversion. It was on a Sunday evening many years ago. And as I stood and listened, I heard him crying out that in the hour when he accepted Christ the sun was different—the moon was different—the flowers in the field were different to him. I thought him a foolish ranter then. I do not think him a foolish ranter now. I remember the gracious word of One who said, "Behold, I make all things new" (2 Cor. 5:17). For in all the great experiences of the soul there is none greater than genuine conversion, and it recreates the faculty of wonder. That is how the rod of God is sometimes sweet and blessed as the dew. It touches the dusty lanes of common life, and they sparkle as on a morning in the May time. The world is never more beautiful or fresh, nor life more wonderful, nor loved ones dearer than after a season when the sky was darkened, and we thought that everything was over.

Now when we turn to Christ, there is one question that naturally rises. Did Christ acknowledge the faculty of wonder? To that question there can be only one answer. There was a lecture the other evening from Professor Milligan[8] on the discoveries that have been lately made in Egypt. Among these discoveries, as he informed you, are certain sayings attributed to Christ. And one of the most beautiful of all of them is this, "he that wonders shall reign, and he that reigns shall rest." Think of it. Inscribe it on your hearts. I feel quite certain it is a genuine saying. Who but Christ would have said in such an age, *he that wonders shall reign, and he that reigns shall rest*? And even as I hear it, I hear another saying—not recovered from Egyptian refuse—"except ye become as little children, ye cannot see the kingdom" (Matt. 18:3). The Pharisee was far too proud to wonder; the little child is wondering all the time. For a child the world is not full of laws and maxims; it is "full of a lot of wonderful things," as Stevenson puts it. And so when Christ dislodged the Pharisee and placed in the center the disregarded child, he proclaimed to everybody with ears to hear, "he that wonders shall reign, and he that reigns shall rest."

---

8. George Milligan (1860–1934), Professor at Glasgow University.

"Let others wrangle," says St. Augustine[9]—"let others wrangle, I shall wonder." You can be a genuine Christian without wrangling, but you never can be a Christian without wondering: wondering at the lilies of the field, at the lights and shadows of the summer evening, at the heaven and hell in the heart of every prodigal, and at the love of God victorious on a cross.

I close by suggesting to you a line of thought that you may carry out with you into the world. It is how the gospel, steadily and surely, has deepened the sense of wonder in mankind. It has done so largely in two ways.

The first is that our Christian faith has added to the mystery of everything. You and I live in a far more awful universe than that which smiled on the lighthearted Greek. There is not a common word which we can use, such as sin, life, death, love or duty, but has become a thousand times more awful since Jesus moved across the fields of Galilee. For the pagan, life was a brief journey; for the Christian, it is the prelude to eternity. For the pagan, death was a forgetting; for the Christian, it is heaven or it is hell. For the old pagan, sin was venial folly; for the Christian, in the light of Calvary, sin is an infinitely guilty thing in the eyes of a holy and eternal God. It was Goethe[10] who said, thinking of all that, that Christianity is the religion of sorrow. Nothing could be more false. It is a religion of joy and peace and power. And yet the strange thing is that at the very heart of an experienced peace too deep for words, there is a mystery that human kind can never fathom. In the presence of a deepened mystery like that, one cannot argue, but can only wonder. We must cease speaking. We must bow. We must say to our heart, *Keep silence before God.* And that is what the faith of Christ has done, and is doing it has recreated wonder by the mystery which it has found in common words like sin and life and death and love and duty.

The second is that our Christian faith has shown us love at the very heart of everything. And wherever love is, whether in heaven or earth, wonder is never far away. That little child asleep in its mother's arms is to you a very ordinary little mortal. But to its mother what a wonderful child it is and wonderful because she

---

9. Augustine (354-430), bishop of Hippo in North Africa, early church father and philosopher.
10. Johann Wolfgang von Goethe (1749–1832), German writer and philosopher.

loves it so. And so with Christ—once we have learned to love Him and to experience His love to us, there falls a newness of wonder upon everything. God is power—I know that He is power; but He may be power and still leave me cold. God is justice—I know that He is justice, and yet infinite justice can never win my heart. God is love, the world is made in love, and every touch of His hand on me is love—and immediately I cry in adoration, *His name shall be called Wonderful.*

"When his eyes were opened, he saw nothing" (Acts 9:8, R.V.).

7
The Blindness of Vision

Blinded by the flash of light from heaven, the apostle was flung prostrate on the ground. It was then that the Savior said to him, "Saul, Saul, why persecutest thou me?" For a little space his eyes were shut, as eyes instinctively shut in self-defense. That flash of light from heaven would have blinded him had it burst on the unguarded eyeball. And then in a moment or two the apostle rose, and looked around him and scanned the heavens above him. *When his eyes were opened, he saw nothing.* Half an hour before he had seen everything—the road, the palms, the gleaming city walls. Now he saw nothing—no human face nor form—no battlement—no cloud upon the sky. And the singular thing is that this loss of vision, this forfeiting of the sweet sight of things, came to him when his eyes were opened.

Now that is a very remarkable conclusion; we are tempted to say it is absurd. It is so different from what we might have expected as a consequence of the opening of the eyes. There was a young man once, in Old Testament times, who was sorely frightened by an Assyrian army. And the prophet, in pity for him, prayed to God, "Lord, open the young man's eyes that he may see" (2 Kings 6:17). And when the eyes of that young man were opened, he saw a sight to make any coward brave for the mountain was full of the chariots of the Lord. That is the fitting consequence of vision. It reveals to us what we never saw before. It shows us in common hearts unlooked-for things, and in common scenes an undiscovered glory. But here, on the road to Damascus and at midday, it is the very opposite which meets us. When his eyes were opened he saw nothing. The question is, in our own life's experience is there anything analogous to that? Is there any opening of the eyes which leaves us with a vision forfeited? That is worth while pondering a little.

In the first place let us think of nature and of all that the world of nature meant to men once. There was a bygone time when nature was alive, when every wood had its dryad or its faun:

> Rough satyrs danced, and fauns with cloven heel
> From the glad sound would not be absent long.[1]

Such was the outlook of man on nature once. It was all haunted by mysterious life in every spring, in every whispering forest, in every glade where shadows lay and lengthened. The great god Pan was moving with his music where the brooklets and the summer winds were calling, and sometimes he was nearer than they knew. Well, all that of course has had to go. Our increased knowledge has banished it forever. No school child believes in fairies now. There are no fairy-rings in any of the standards? And I suggest, to those who have ears to hear, that there are thousands for whom a little knowledge just means that when their eyes were opened *they saw nothing*.

Putting the matter in another light, suppose we think of the little frets of life, of the little pinpricks and unkindnesses which most people experience as they journey. There are folk who brood upon such things as these until they practically see nothing else. They tend and water all their little grievances until their blossoms would take prizes at a show. And what I have noticed of such folk is that when through the mercy of God their eyes are opened, of all these little pinpricks they see nothing. Their eyes have been opened to what real suffering is. They were only playing before at being miserable. Their eyes have been opened to that larger life which is always given us in Christ. And the beautiful thing about that life is that worries which were overwhelming yesterday somehow have vanished so that we cannot see them in the love commended on the cross. Every rock and ridge is clear and glistening in the

---

1. From "Lycidas," by John Milton (1608–74), English poet.

Highland burn[2] when it is low. But when the summer rain falls or the winter snow, then they become invisible. And I have found it so in many people's lives when a new tide of being has possessed them. Things that were sharp and hard, and hurt yesterday, somehow have become invisible today. "Son, why hast thou thus dealt with us"—they felt the sting of it, and thought that he was unfilial. But when their eyes were opened, *they saw nothing*; that filial ingratitude had vanished. So when we see, many a thing vanishes—many a thing which hurt and fretted us, met us everywhere, barred the sunshine out, and silenced all the music in the dwelling.

Does not the same thing often happen also with that opening of the eyes which the years bring? We experience it in many different ways. Here, for instance, is a child who thinks the world of a certain picture. It hangs on the wall of the nursery at home and is perfectly beautiful to him. It is only a rough and in artistic daub—a crude, gaudy, glaring oleograph—but to the child it is a joy forever. Then the years pass, and the little brain is educated. These two little eyes are taught to see—taught to distinguish what is really beautiful from what is only a travesty of beauty. And then the child comes back to that old oleograph which long ago was a very heaven of gladness; now that its eyes are opened, *it sees nothing*. We can mark our progress by our growing vision.

We can also mark it by our growing blindness. Not only do we see more as the years pass; if we are spending them rightly, we see less—less in certain books we thought the world of, and in certain societies we held delightful, in certain characters we thought ideal. How many a wildly infatuated girl has had the experience of our text. In spite of the warnings of a mother's love, she insisted on idealizing somebody, and perhaps she married him. Then her eyes were opened in the long dusty highway to Damascus. When her eyes were opened *she saw nothing*—nothing of the manhood she had dreamed, nothing of the strength that she had conjured; nothing but selfishness where she had looked for service; nothing but coldness where she had looked for love. May heaven be very merciful to such on the desert road when the ideal has vanished, for it is always a perilous season on life's journey.

Then our text, as it seems to me, applies again to many of those

---

2. a brook or small stream

messages with which the world is ringing. There are faiths and philosophies which vanish when you see. When the sun is shining on you and the world is beautiful, you go, for instance, to hear a certain preacher. You have never been plunged into the depths yet and have never felt your utter need of Christ. And the man is artistic or he is intellectual or he has the fire and passion of the orator, and you feel as if you would never want another message. My brother, if the sun were always shining, it may be that such a message would be sufficient. But this is a strange, grim world with lightning-flashes and storms that cry havoc, and waves that cruelly beat. And when these days come, and you feel your need of Christ, and of an arm to lean on and a hand to save you, no charm of speech—no intellect nor artistry—can reach and grip and satisfy the soul. You want a power to hold you out of hell. You want a love that goes unto the uttermost. You want a heart on which to lean securely though the whole universe should fall in ruin. And whenever through trial and suffering and sorrow your eyes have been opened to see that, then in the fine artistic preaching *you see nothing*. Nothing to pluck you from the miry clay. Nothing commensurate with sin and hell. Nothing that can be heard across the battle, like the voice of the trumpet summoning to victory. That is why the old and chastened saints, who have suffered and struggled, battled, conquered, fallen, feel sometimes that there is not a word for them in preaching which may be exquisite as music.

I want also to say in passing that our text has got another application. It applies to the recognition which we give to people—too late. I think of two, long centuries ago, who were joined by a third as they journeyed to Emmaus. And though He opened the Scriptures to them until their hearts were burning, their eyes were holden and they did not know Him. And then they invited Him in to share their evening meal, and in the breaking of the bread their eyes were opened, they knew Him, and He vanished from their sight. When their eyes were opened, they saw nothing. The One who was all the world to them was gone. *There* was the cup He had drunk from in their company, and there the couch on which He had reclined. O, son or daughter, here in this church tonight, with a mother who loves you with all a mother-love, see that your recognition of her presence be not a gazing at vacancy like that. You take her as a matter of course this evening. Your eyes are blind; you do not recognize. You do not dream what pleasure you could give by a little self-sacrifice for her who loves you so. I bid you awaken, while the days are flying, lest when it is all too late and you are motherless, your eyes should be terribly opened and *see nothing*.

I close by suggesting that in the case of Paul, and in the case of many a people since Paul, this is what happens when through the Holy Ghost our eyes are opened to see that we are sinners. There was a Pharisee once who came up to the Temple, and he thanked God he was not as other men. He fasted and was an exemplary person; he was proud of all he was and all he did. In that same temple was a publican whose eyes had been opened by the grace of God, and when his eyes were opened, *he saw nothing*. Nothing of all his fasting and his tithing; nothing of all he had ever striven to do. His best was sinful. His life had been a failure. "God be merciful to me a sinner" (Luke 18:13). My brother, when you see nothing, you see Christ. When you see that your best is rags, you see His riches. When you see at last that you have nothing to plead, you are ready for all the gladness of His grace.

"I the Lord thy God am a jealous God"
(Ex. 20:5).

8
The Jealousy of God

Jealousy is so associated with evil that we hesitate to attribute it to God. We should never have ventured to think of God as jealous without the authority of Holy Scripture. A jealous nature in a man or woman is not one that commands our admiration. We do not despise it as we do a mean nature, but we certainly do not admire it. And all our associations with the word, gathered from the experience of life, create in us an instinct of recoil from attributing jealousy to God. Among the passions portrayed for us by Shakespeare there is one unrivaled portraiture of jealousy. Jealousy is the absorbing passion, as it is the ruin, of Othello.[1] And so inwrought into the minds of students is that unrivaled creation of the dramatist, that it has tended to color the jealousy of God. Here is a nature essentially great, goaded into the madness of a beast. There is in Othello a certain grand simplicity such as is always found in noble natures. And yet Othello becomes blind and mad and ends by murdering the woman whom he worshiped under the overmastering power of jealousy. It is such things that make Bacon[2] in his *Essays* speak of envy as the vilest of all passions. It

---
1. From *Othello* by William Shakespeare.
2. Francis Bacon (1561–1626), English philosopher and essayist.

distorts everything, blinds the vision, and is the mother of profound unhappiness. And that is why we naturally shrink, as our experience of life increases, from attributing the passion of jealousy to God.

Nor is the Bible, to which we owe the thought, ignorant of that darker side of jealousy. Like Shakespeare, it has wonderful portraiture of jealous men in its picture gallery. There is Cain, for instance, on the verge of history, madly jealous of his brother Abel. There is Saul, who was not unlike Othello in a certain heroic simplicity of nature. And yet when the women cried in the day of victory, "Saul hath slain his thousands and David his ten thousands" (1 Sam. 18:7), the heart of the kingly Saul was turned to bitterness. He who could fight like a lion in the battle could not tolerate his rival's eminence. It was as gall and wormwood to his spirit that David should have the precedence in praise. He missed that crowning touch of our own Nelson[3] who, when the fleets were closing at Trafalgar, said, "See that gallant fellow Collingwood, how he carries his ship into action."

Then when we turn to the New Testament, we find there also an ample recognition. We have it in the disciples when they forbade the man who was casting out devils in the name of Christ. We have it also in the Scribes and Pharisees who were so madly jealous of the Master that nothing would satisfy them but His death. The jealousy of neighboring towns or villages is too notorious to be disputed. Well, in Galilee there were two neighboring villages, of which the one was Cana and the other Nazareth. And it illuminates the page of Scripture to remember that it was Nathanael of Cana who asked the bitter and derisive question, "Can any good come out of *Nazareth*?" (John 1:46). We do not need to turn to Shakespeare, then, to apprehend the darker side of jealousy. In all its tragedy and all its pettiness, it is known and registered in Holy Scripture. And yet the Bible, which knows our human hearts and searches out the latent evil in them, assures us of the jealousy of God.

We begin to see the solution of this difficulty when we recall the connection of jealousy with love. Jealousy is the shadow cast by love. That is, indeed, in our common speech, the difference between jealousy and envy. For envy, as it is the meaner word, so is it

---

3. Horatio (Viscount) Nelson (1758–1805), English admiral.

also by far the broader word. It applies to the intellect as well as to the heart, to ambitions as well as to affections, and to relationships where love is never thought of. One scholar may be envious of another, and one actor may be envious of another. But in our common speech we do not say that a husband is envious of his wife. We say that a husband is jealous of his wife, because marriage is a relationship of love. That is why we speak of Cain as jealous—because he and Abel had once loved each other. That is why we speak of Saul as jealous—because his heart had been knit to that of David. And even the disciples, when they forbade the man, were not envious of rival power; they were jealous because they loved their Lord. We may be envious of other people although it has never been our lot to love them. But an indifferent wife cannot be jealous; she only becomes jealous when she loves. And so in human life, as witnessed in our speech, jealousy is one side of love, though often a very dark and tragic side. It is along such lines that we begin to fathom the possibility of jealousy in God. For the God of the Bible in His essential nature is revealed to us as Love. And if that love flows out upon humanity in an infinite and everlasting mercy, it also, if it is deep and mighty, can scarcely lack the attribute of jealousy.

Nor is there any spiritual peril in thus attributing jealousy to God. For it is God alone who has the right to the undivided devotion of the creature. That is where human jealousy is evil. That is the source of all its bitter tragedy. It is the passionate claim of one poor human creature to the undivided devotion of another. And however noble such a claim may be, as witnessing the fervor of affection, it is always selfish and forever wrong. No human heart is large or deep enough entirely to absorb another heart. We are all finite creatures at our highest; and one such creature cannot fill another. And so our jealousy tends to become sinful, because it is our assertion of a claim that is proper to the infinity of God. For only God can satisfy the heart—even the poorest and the meanest heart. Only He can absorb it without wronging it, for in Him we live and move and have our being. Only He has the full right to say in the highest spiritual interest of His children, "My son, give me your heart." Radically, therefore, the jealousy of God does not differ from the jealousy of man. They are alike in this, that both are born of love—a love that cannot tolerate a rival. But the jealousy of man grows dark and terrible because it makes a claim that is impossible, and the jealousy of God makes it *of right*.

How closely associated the divine love and jealousy are, is witnessed in a very simple way. It is in the Bible, and the Bible only, that we meet with the thought of the jealousy of God. That the unseen powers are envious of man is one of the oldest conceptions of the race. You light on it far back in ancient Greece; you detect it in a hundred superstitions. That the gods are envious and always on the watch and filled with a bitter grudge against too great prosperity is one of the oldest conceptions of the human mind. I need hardly point out to you that such divine envy is wholly different from divine jealousy. It does not spring from a great pity; it springs from the malevolence of spite. And not until there had dawned upon the world that truth so wonderful—that God is love—do you ever have the truth that God is jealous. That is why you find it in the Bible and find it nowhere else than in the Bible. It is the Bible and the Bible only that has convinced the world that God is love. And it is the very depth and splendor of that love, sealed in the gift of the Lord Jesus Christ, which has given us the jealousy of God.

I want you to note again that the same attitude is very evident in our Lord Himself. It is something we are apt to overlook. As we recall how Jesus walked in mercy, we lift up our hearts assured that God is merciful. As we remember His compassion for the fallen, we are filled with the certainty that God is love. But no one can read the story of the gospels, believing that God was incarnate in humanity, without awaking to the awful truth that the Lord our God is a jealous God. As surely as God will tolerate no rival, Jesus Christ would tolerate no rival. He makes a claim upon the human heart of absolute and unconditional surrender. Even had we never heard from the Old Testament that there was such a thing as divine jealousy, we should conclude it from the life of Jesus. There were many things which Jesus tolerated which we should never have thought to find Him tolerating. He bore with social abuses—with personal discourtesies—in a way that is sometimes hard to understand.

But there was one thing Jesus *never* tolerated, from the first hour of His calling to the last, and that was the division of His empire. "No man cometh to the Father but by me" (John 14:6). "All judgment has been committed to the Son" (John 5:22). "I am the way; I am the truth; I am the life" (John 14:6). "No man knoweth the

The Jealousy of God

Father but the Son" (Matt. 11:27). That is either the most stupendous arrogance which was ever listened to from human lips—or else it is the jealousy of God. That the Lord our God, then, is a jealous God, is abundantly evident in Jesus Christ. It is more plainly written in the Incarnate Word than in any reason annexed to the commandment. And it is well we should remember that when we are tempted to presume upon that Fatherhood which is infinitely merciful and kind.

This deep thought of the jealousy of God has been powerfully influential in two ways. It has, in the first place, given tremendous impulse to the vital doctrine of monotheism. It has been of supreme importance to the race to learn the lesson that God is one. All spiritual progress has depended on it; all true knowledge has depended on it. And that great doctrine, so vital to humanity, has been tremendously deepened in appeal by the truth that rang out to Israel, "The Lord thy God is a jealous God." The first thing that had to be impressed on men was that the worship of many gods was quite intolerable. They must be taught that for reasons yet unknown to them it was infinitely offensive to the Lord. And it was taught, sublimely and yet simply, to men who as yet were spiritually children by the ascription of jealousy to God. It is not easy for you and me today to appreciate the attraction of polytheism. Yet every reader of the Old Testament knows how tremendous were its attractions to the Jew. And if the office and calling of the Jews was to give to humanity the truth that God is one, do you not see that some mighty thought was needed to keep them true to their spiritual leading? That mighty thought was the jealousy of God: "The Lord thy God is a jealous God." It burned itself into the heart of Israel that God would tolerate no rival claim. And thus, not without many a lapse, was the world led to that profound conviction without which there is no unity nor peace.

That thought, lastly, has been very powerful in making ready for the incarnation. It is really the herald—the strange and shadowy herald—of the love that has been revealed in Jesus Christ. A jealous God may be a dark conception, but a jealous God can never be indifferent. When love is jealous it may do cruel deeds, but at least it is a love intense and passionate. And so in the Old Testament you seem to find divine sanction for very cruel deeds; but you never find a God who does not care. He loves with a love so burning and intense that He is passionately jealous for His people. "He who toucheth you," He cries to them, "toucheth the apple of mine eye" (Zech. 2:8). And it was that great love, purged of its grosser elements and shown in a beauty that man had never dreamed of, that was at last revealed in the Lord Jesus Christ. The jealousy of God is the true key to some of the darkest deeds in the Old Testament. But do not forget that it also is the key to the coming of the Lord and Savior. For it tells of a love so deep and strong and wonderful that it will go at last to any length of sacrifice—even to the giving of His Son.

"Better is a dinner of herbs where love is,
than a stalled ox and hatred therewith"
(Prov. 15:17).

9
The Contentment of Love

I like to think that Solomon wrote these words as a result of personal observation. I like to think of him like that Eastern caliph, moving abroad with his tablets by his side. No man could ever have written this book of Proverbs, however instructed of the Holy Ghost, unless he had watched with all-observing eyes the lights and shadows of humanity. And the deep proof that his watching was inspired by the great Spirit which broods upon mankind is just that his wise sayings are still valid. To pierce through the seeming to the real—to penetrate from accident to essence—that is a work which calls for more than cleverness; it calls for the light of the candle of the Lord. And so one mark of an inspired Scripture is just that it rings true through all the centuries, when the men and women who first heard the oracle are turned to dust and ashes in their graves.

And so I like to think that Solomon here wrote with some concrete instance in his memory and that we have a transcript here of what he had actually seen with his own eyes. It is not easy for a king to see things as they are. There is a conspiracy to hide reality from kings. Even your sordid slum is decked and bannered when majesty is announced to pass that way. And banners hide far more than they display, and triumphal arches are a sorry business for the one triumphal arch for any king is the lowly doorway of his people's homes. So Solomon, unattended, unescorted, had gone out one evening through the city gates. And there he had seen a laborer coming home, wearied with the toiling of the day. And his little child had come running out to meet him, and his wife had given him welcome at the door. Then in the humble cottage, safe and happy, they had sat down together at their meal. Then Solomon thought of his state banquets, where the viands[1] were costly and where the music played. And he thought of the envious hearts and hates and jealousies that festered in the circles of the court. And then he took his tablet from his side and, touched with a wistfulness that even kings may feel, wrote, "Better is a dinner of herbs where love is, than a stalled ox and hatred therewith."

Thus the monarch was through that day's experience brought face to face with a great living truth. He saw, as he had never seen before, that love is the secret of contentment. Solomon had everything the world could give him. He was dowered with the infinite riches of the earth. For him there were argosies[2] on many a sea and traffickers in many a distant market. And Tyrian purple was with him as nothing, and the gold of Ophir was a common element, and the one thing which he lacked in all his glory was the priceless blessing of a contented heart. There is a contentment which is the child of cowardice: it is the dull submission of the broken-spirited. There is the sad contentment of the dying when the lamp of life is flickering to extinction.

But the contentment which the Bible preaches is not any dull and heavy-eyed submission: it is the contentment which is full of gladness because it rests its head upon the lap of love. "Better a dinner of herbs where love is, than a stalled ox and hatred therewith." Where love is, nothing matters very much. We are not dependent upon a golden summer. Loveless, a man may fly to Switzerland and think to find in Switzerland his paradise. But he who dwells in love dwells in the center and finds his kingdom and paradise at home.

Of course, it is the strange paradox of love that it is also the

---

1. choice foods
2. a fleet of merchant ships

mother of a great discontent. Love is content because it *believeth* all things and yet is never content because it *hopeth* all things. I knew a woman, the wife of a humble farmer, who had three or four sons about her feet. And when the fare was meager, as it often was, she used to quote this text to the young savages. And yet that woman, just because she loved them, was heroically and divinely discontented, until she had raised them up to a manhood of preeminence. All her rest was in her mother's love for them, and yet that love was magnificently restless. And she taught herself Latin that she might hear their lessons and spurred them to the desire for college learning. And all of them became an honor to their country and rose up in the gate to call her blessed and dwelt with infinite fondness in old age on the early love that would not let them go. Love is the mother of all discontent. It has hopes that burn more brightly than a star. It is restless with all the restlessness of God who elaborates a people to His praise. And yet like God it is infinitely restful and can go singing down the meanest street, and can find in a few herbs a royal banquet that is richer than the prodigality of kings.

We see that in every sphere of life, wherever what we call love is operative, for love at the heart of it is always *one*, whatever be the object of desire. I had the privilege a week or two ago of having a day's yachting with a friend. Fortunately it was a very calm day, and my friend assured me it was a beautiful yacht. Well, down a ladder in a dark and curious cavern there was something which he told me was a bed. I have no doubt I should have slept on it quite soundly, if my good doctor had given me one of these medications we hear of. And not far from the bed there was a stove which I was assured was a marvel of a stove, and from which, to do my friend all justice, he produced a liquid which he designated tea. Now that dear friend of mine, who will forgive me should he happen to be in our audience tonight—that dear friend of mine is a born sailor and loves yachting to the finest fiber of his being.

And so did I find myself, under the purpling hills and amid the silent waters of Loch Striven, whispering to myself this ancient oracle, "Better is a dinner of herbs where love is." All the appointments of his father's house, the successive courses of its table, the silent waiting of perfectly trained service and the snowy sheets in the chamber toward the sun-rising—all these were not for a moment to be matched with the coarse fare and bedding of the *Red-*

wing, because its owner was a born lover of the sea. That is always the joy of the born lover. A dish of herbs becomes to him a banquet. He does not wait for the sunshine to be happy, nor for the villa, nor for the motorcar. He can be happy in the meanest lodging, fired, it may be, with a divine unrest, yet filled, just because God is love, with the unutterable rest of God.

Doubtless the secret of that great contentment lies partly in the power of love to see. We have a proverb that says that love is blind, but true love has the keenest of all sight. Love is always generous in interpreting, seeing what to others is invisible, finding a worshiping woman in a Magdalene and a kingdom of heaven in a grain of mustard. Your worldling whose only god is money will tell you contemptuously that love is worth zero. But he of all men should know the power of a zero in multiplying the units into thousands. I take a zero that he despises and write them down after the figure one, and I have changed my one into a million. There is a beautiful Oriental legend of how a dead dog was flung into the marketplace. And the merchants shrank from it in sheer disgust and said, "Faugh, what an ugly brute, and how it smells!" And then someone moved across the square, saw it lying, halted for an instant, and then said very quietly to his comrades, "Pearls could not equal the whiteness of its teeth." Hatred can see nothing but a carcass. Love has always eyes for the white teeth. It sees a Peter strong as mountain-rock in the character that is shifty as the sand. It sees a possible tomorrow in midnight, a possible hero in an actual prodigal, and in a dinner of herbs at eventide a banquet fit for the palace of a king.

Contentment does not spring from what you have; contentment always springs from what you see. You can use a penny to give a beggar bread, or you can use it to shut out the sun. And that is why love is infinitely happy, because it sees with the very eyes of God and finds, as Jesus found when He was here, "infinite riches in a little room." Your little boy comes to you on your birthday, and he says, "Father, I've painted a nice picture for you." And you look at it, and with considerable difficulty you recognize what he tells you is a horse. The coloring is not exactly that of Rubens,[3] nor does the scenery suggest this habitable planet, and yet that little picture is more precious to you than any of the old masters in the gallery. And

---

3. Peter Paul Rubens (1577–1640), Flemish painter.

The Contentment of Love

you put it away in that locked drawer of yours where there lie those letters in a girlish hand. And the birthday passes, and you go back to business and probably forget that it is there. But some day long hence you will light upon it, and in that day it will be wet with tears, as you think of the dear dead days beyond recall. It is the giver makes the gift precious. When we love the giver, we always love the gift. Better a poor, rough daub by a little hand we loved than the "Last Judgment" of a Michaelangelo. Better a dinner of herbs that love has served and where we sit in the fellowship of those who love us than all the delicacies the world can furnish where there are no hearts to answer ours.

And that is why, when we dwell in the love of God, we win the blessing of a great repose. To live in God is always to be restless, and yet to live in God is perfect rest. It is one thing to be content with what we *are*; it is another to be content with what we *have*. The one is a certain sign of spiritual death; the other is a certain sign of love. So he who dwells in God knows the strange paradox of growing more discontented with himself yet always growing into a new content with the lot that has been appointed him by heaven. How profoundly dissatisfied with his religious progress was the greatest and most heroic of apostles! "O wretched man that I am," Paul cries in agony, "who shall deliver me from this body of death?" (Rom. 7:24). Yet that apostle, from a Roman prison, could lift his heart to heaven in adoration, and cry, "I have learned in whatsoever state I am, therewith to be content" (Phil. 4:11). Profoundly dissatisfied with what he was, he was profoundly satisfied with what he had. Divinely discontented with himself, he was divinely contented with his lot. And that has ever been one happy feature of the gospel which has rung out the grace of God; it has given the sweet contentment of true love.

I have a dear friend who, when she was a girl, used to collect for charities in Ayrshire. And one of the cottages she had to visit was that of a pious and reverent old woman. Betty was in very straitened circumstances, so much so that no one knew how she existed, yet would she have been mightily insulted if the collector had dared to pass her door. One day, when the collector visited the cottage, Betty was sitting at her tea. And as she rose to get her widow's mite out of the chest, she threw her apron hastily across the tea-table. Whereon the girl, in girlish curiosity, lifted the apron to see what it concealed and found that the hidden cup was filled with water. "Why,

Betty," she cried in her astonishment, "it isn't tea you've got here, it is water." "Ay, my dear," said Betty, "it's just water, but *He makes it taste like wine*." Better a cup of water where love is, than choicest vintage of the grape without it. "Better a dinner of herbs where love is, than a stalled ox where there is hatred." Nor is there any love of man so deep and broad, so perfect in its power and in its tenderness, as the love of God that is commended to us in the death of our Lord and Savior Jesus Christ.

"But Peter continued knocking"
(Acts 12:16).

10
The Grace of Continuance

It is perilous to judge a person by one action. Life is too complex and intricate for that. It is as if one were to judge a countryside by a single and isolated clump of trees. Ruskin has it that if out of a Turner landscape you cut a quarter of an inch of sky, within that single quarter of an inch you would feel the infinity of heaven. It may be there are lives like that, so penetrated with purpose or with passion, that wherever you touch them you get the real character. As a general rule, however, it is a perilous thing to judge a man by any single action. In his great hours he may be greater than himself; possibly he may be less than his true self. And always it is wisest, if you would judge a person not by the tenor of his life but by an action, to take an action of a usual kind. There was an hour, for instance, when Peter drew his sword and cut off the ear of the priest's servant with it. There was another hour—never to be forgotten—when, panic-stricken, he denied his Lord. But if I wished to know the real Peter, I should not turn to either of these hours; I should rather choose an action such as this—*Peter continued knocking*. Shall I tell you what it reveals in the apostle? Three things that are well worth observing.

In the first place, this common act shows Peter's *courage*. It makes that unmistakable. Whoever it was who stood there in the street, it was not a panic-stricken man. When Peter broke prison we know what hour it was; it was the fourth watch of the night. This indicates that it was no longer dark; the day was beginning to glimmer in the east. The smoke of the household fires was mounting heavenward, and the first footfalls were echoing on the pavements, *and Peter continued knocking.* Shrouded in the darkness of the third watch, he might have been reasonably safe out in the street. But in the fourth watch, when the sun was rising, it was at his peril that he delayed a moment. Yet Peter, who had once been panic-stricken and in an agony of fear denied his Lord, was evidently not panic-stricken now. It was a very usual thing to do, and yet it was a courageous thing to do, far more courageous than that whirling passion which plucked the sword out of the scabbard once. And it sprang from the certainty that God was with him and, having rescued him, would not desert him now. "The Lord will perfect that which concerneth me" (Ps. 138:8).

Now that is a lesson we would do well to learn about the essential quality of courage. Just to continue knocking patiently may be braver than the most gallant deed. I grant you there come moments in our lives when courage may flash into dramatic splendor. There are hours for men of crowded life which are worth an age without a name. When the soldier moves forward to save a wounded comrade—when the fireman risks his life to save a child—when the six hundred as at Balaclava ride into the very jaws of death—there is something in that which strangely moves the heart.

But that is the courage which is thrilling rather than the courage which is telling. The truest courage in this life of ours is seldom momentary or spectacular. It moves in the shadow of the dreary street and dwells in the dull seclusion of the home; it continues doing things, with quiet heart, when the natural impulse would be to turn and flee. Just to get up each dull and dreary morning and say, "Please, God, I shall play my part today." Just to go out and do it quietly in the teeth of wearinesses and ingratitudes, just to shut our ears to calling voices and bear our daily cross victoriously is the finest heroism on this side the river. No man is ever far from the heroic who has learned to do things when he feels least like them. There is little hope for a man in this strange world who surrenders to his whimsies every morning. To trample under foot all moods and feelings—to get to our duty and our cross in

The Grace of Continuance

spite of them—to do *that* summer and winter until we die is the one road to the music and the crown. That was preeminently true of Christ. His was the courage of continuance. Through ridicule, through rebuke, through suffering, Christ continued knocking.

In the second place, this common action reveals to us Peter's *understanding*. Clearly he did not misinterpret what was happening within the house. Contrast him, for instance, with Naaman. When Naaman was bidden go and wash in Jordan, he thought that the prophet was making light of him. So Naaman turned and went away in a rage because he misinterpreted the prophet. And if Peter had misinterpreted like that, he too would have gone away in a great rage; but *Peter continued knocking*. We are always ready for misinterpretation when we knock or ring at a door and no one answers, doubly ready when we see peering faces behind the glass of the door or through the blind. And that is precisely what Peter had to bear, for Rhoda came and looked and went away again, and yet Peter understood it perfectly.

The fact is he understood their feelings by what had happened that morning to himself. That is always how we understand people: by the kind of thing which has happened to ourselves. Half an hour earlier Peter had seen an angel, and he had been dazed and thought it was a ghost; and now *they* think that Peter is a ghost, and Peter instantly grasps the situation. That is why he did not grow indignant. That is why he did not stalk away. He understood from his own stupefaction how terrified they would be for a few moments. And so he stood there, out in the street at daybreak, and continued knocking, and showed by his action that he understood.

Is it not usually in that way that people come to know we understand them? "Though I speak with the tongue of men and of angels, and have not charity, it profiteth me nothing" (1 Cor. 13:1, 3). To be misunderstood is a true grief. It is a grief which Christ experienced to the full. A man is never himself—never at his best—when he is surrounded by misunderstanding. But when a man feels that he is understood, he casts aside reserve and is himself, and he generally feels that through common touches. There are people who would give their bodies to be burned, and yet you never feel they understand. There are others who do no splendid services and yet have a genius for understanding. By a kindly question, by a homely word, by a little deed of kindness light as gossamer, men waken to find that they are understood. All great leaders of men have had that gift. It is really the secret of personal attraction. No power of organizing mighty armies will ever explain Napoleon, for example. Along with that must be the touch which tells and the mystic sympathy that breaks down strangerhood, if dying legionaries are to cry "My Emperor." If you can serve in great and splendid ways, then go and serve thus, and the Lord reward you. If you have genius or have wealth, consecrate them all to noble causes. But if you can only do quite common kindnesses, do not neglect them while the days are hurrying for they tell men that they are understood.

Then, in the third place, this common action reveals to us Peter's *consecration*. He stood there knocking—and half an hour before he had been in the royal company of angels. It is all very well for a beggar to stand and knock. A doorstep may be a beggar's proper place. But Peter had had an experience that morning which had lifted him up into the courts of heaven. He had been made a little lower than the angels, for he had had an angel for his visitor; and yet in the dawn out in the common street *Peter continued knocking*. A little while before, that very morning, Peter had come to a great iron gate. And at a single touch of the angelic finger that gate had opened to let Peter through. And now he was at no massive iron gate but at the humble door of a very humble dwelling—and he continued knocking.

Had this chapter been a medieval legend, you would have had that cottage door fly open also. But the Book of Acts is no Arabian Nights; it is true to experience, and it is true to character. For sometimes the massive gates which we have dreaded, at the touch of God fly open when we reach them, and the little doors are the hardest to get through. That is why I say a touch like this shows Peter as a consecrated man. He had been exalted up to heaven, and difficulties had vanished from his path. And now he was back again among life's obstacles and the street doors that everybody knows— and he continued knocking.

Now unquestionably, as it was with Peter, so is it with every one of us. There is no such certain mark of consecration as just to return like that to common levels. We too, like Peter, have our hours of vision. We have our seasons when the heavens are opened. We have our mornings when we see the angels in the light that never was on sea or land. It may be in church; it may be in the country; it

The Grace of Continuance

may be when love comes in and sings her music; or it may be when some one very dear is taken, and the heart is emptier than the home. In such an hour as that we are like Peter. The angels are never far away. In such an hour as that, whether for weal or woe, we see our visions, and we dream our dreams.

And then we have to go back to common doors, where there is no mystery of blood upon the lintel, and the question is what shall we do then? There are some who are too unsettled to do anything. They could have knocked yesterday; they cannot knock today. They have lost all interest in common tasks, and the dreary round of duty is unbearable. But he who is consecrated as Simon Peter was, through the pardoning and restoring love of Christ—he *will continue knocking*. He will be a better father to his children. He will be a more caring brother to his sisters. Deepened by sorrow, purified by love, he will go with a faithful heart to his day's drudgery. He will continue knocking until the door shall open, and faces that he has loved will answer his in a fellowship where time and space are not.

"I lifted up mine eyes again, and looked, and behold a man [a young man, v.4] with a measuring line in his hand. Then said I, Whither goest thou? And he said unto him, To measure Jerusalem" (Zech. 2:1–2).

11

The Young Man with the Measuring Line

This is one of the visions of the prophet in the place where he regularly went to pray. It is one of the most suggestive of them all. Zechariah had come back from Babylon in the company of the returning exiles. There was no glory about that return, such as Isaiah had pictured so magnificently. They were despondent and they were spiritless. They were leaving a land of sunshine and of wealth. With dragging footsteps they made their weary way to a desolate city and a ruined temple. It is in such hours that great men show themselves. Like pillars of fire they burn amid the shadows. Others are hopeless and let the hands hang down, but the heroic heart still has its visions. And so these Jewish patriots and heroes, whom we disguise under the name of prophets, roused the people, kept hope aflame, and urged them to the rebuilding of the ruins.

And so one night while his compatriots slept, Zechariah stole out to the valley to pray. And there, as he prayed among the myrtle trees, he saw the shadowy figure of a man. In his right hand he held a measuring line; he was a fellow of the great Society of Measurers. And being such, we learn without surprise that to the watching prophet he seemed *young*. Had he been old and limping through the valley with the moonlight shining upon his silvered hair, it is not a measuring line he would have carried but a line of pity and of ignorance. Ripe old age ceases to measure things. It leaves all that to an omniscient God. It has found there are more things in heaven and earth than are dreamed of in our philosophy. But youth, with that supreme audacity which is one of the choicest fruits of lack of wisdom, will measure everything and everybody and in half an hour will pigeonhole the universe. That is why, if I am not mistaken, the prophet saw a *young* man in this vision. Every exact measurer is young, which is to say that he is inexperienced. As the years pass we find that thirty yards may be longer than thirty million miles, and that all the leagues between heaven and hell may be reduced to the compendium of an inch.

And so the young man passed across the valley, and the prophet asked him what he was going to do. Whereon he answered with an engaging frankness that he was going to measure Jerusalem, as if a ragged urchin with a whistle should set himself to play an oratorio. Measure Jerusalem, just think of it! Measure the city of the living God! Set down on a paper, in yards and feet and inches, all that is gathered in that word *Jerusalem*—all the tears that have been wept in it—all the songs that have been sung in it—all the crying of brokenhearted men in it that had gone quivering to the ear of God. There are some things in life you cannot measure. Their meaning and their value are immeasurable. Tell me their area, and you have told me nothing. Their value is not of space but of the spirit, of noble memories that cling to them, of heroisms that turn their dust to gold, of trust in God and conquest of the devil, that make their trifling area like paradise. No wonder this young man was stopped and stopped with the swift authority of heaven. To measure anything with God in it is one of the most hopeless of employments. It is to misinterpret all the past and to bedim the promise of the future which pulses with a hope that is incalculable and thrills with the possibilities of heaven.

It is well we should remember this in regard to the surroundings of a man. The verdict of the measuring line is worthless. Here is a student in his city lodging which even his landlady could not describe as spacious. There is room to eat in it, room to sleep in it, and room for a book or two and for a photograph. But in these thrilling days of student liberty, when the heart is bounding and the brain is busy, the height of it and the depth of it are ampler than all the splendid proportions of a palace. I measure a nursery not by lineal inches—I measure a nursery by the love of children. I measure a library not by its thousand volumes—I measure it by its inspiration. And so I sometimes find the meanest library long as time and broad as the whole universe and the richest of them the size of a French novel.

I remember once when I was in Stratford-on-Avon seeing a very remarkable sight. It was a man in the street, outside the house of Shakespeare, busy with his theodolite.[1]

Even then, though I was not religious and not much given to finding Bible parallels, I remember how I was tempted to accost him and ask him if he was measuring Jerusalem. So many cubic feet in Shakespeare's house—so many palaces of Elsinore! So many toiling domestics in the kitchen—so many Ariels and Calibans! And all the villainy of Iago in it, and all the love of Romeo and Juliet, and all the sighing of melancholy Jacques in the forest that is everywhere and nowhere.[2] When you go down to Alloway to see the cottage there, you had better leave your measuring line behind you. If you do not, you will be disappointed, for some of you could put that cottage in your drawing room. And yet, if I might venture to suggest, it is a larger place than many drawing rooms where there is watered tea, watered cleverness, and everything watered but the heart. Give me love, and the cottage is a palace. Give me a mother, and you give me home. And the heart will return to it and visit it in yearning and clothe it in the gladsomeness of paradise. All which it is well to bear in mind when we think that the last secret of the universe is the fact that twelve inches make a foot, and three feet make a yard.

The same divine rejection of the measuring line is often necessary in regard to Scripture. It is the proper attitude of every earnest man who looks on the Scripture as a living thing. I have known

---

1. an early surveying instrument
2. All references to characters and scenes from Shakespeare's plays.

certain estimable people who looked on the Scripture as a box of tools. Well, of course, if it is a box of tools, you can take its measurements immediately; it is just so many inches high, and just so many inches broad, and there is a nice little padlock on the lid for which these worthy people have the key. Out with these desecrating figures! The word of God is not a box of tools. The word of God is a breathing, living thing. It lives and abides forever. The word of the living God is a *seed*, and he who wants to measure a seed rightly has more to do than measure its dimensions. I take a tiny seed upon my hand—our Savior would call it a grain of mustard seed; and then, with all laborious exactitude, I find it measures the thousandth of an inch. And I record that fact upon my notebook and then communicate it to the scientific papers, and weary toilers lift their heads and say, "Thank God for another accurate observer." Meantime the seed is cast into the soil and, unobserved, a miracle is happening. It is springing up and bursting its integument[3] and claiming its glorious kinship with the sun. And the birds of heaven are lodging in its branches, and it is green and beautiful and shadowy; and yet of all that miracle there was no reckoning in the exact and scientific measurement.

Now I am not an enemy of biblical criticism. I am a Scotsman and, I trust, a student. I want the truth about the word of God though it should shatter many a boyish fancy. But with deepening intensity I feel that when you have laid all human measurements on Scripture, you may have missed the wonder of it and the miracle and the living power that makes it what it is. Tell me that there were two Isaiahs; I am willing to believe that there were ten. Tell me that Moses never wrote a line; I can reply that neither did our Savior. Measure the seed. Measure the Word of God. Measure it accurately and scientifically. But in the living germinating power of it I am confronted by a thing that is immeasurable. I do not reckon the seed by its integument. I reckon it by the glory of the harvest. And to me the Scripture is not a thing of chapters. It is a living power in kinship with the heavens. I think of all the men that it has helped. I think of all the women it has blessed. I think of the weeping eyes that it has dried and of the broken hearts that it has comforted. My highly intellectual friend, leave your measuring line at home sometimes. Leave it at home—it is cumber-

---

3. a covering or enclosure

some to carry; go out freehanded to wonder and adore. And perhaps Jerusalem will live for you, and the word of God will reach you unexpectedly, and you will find in it more than you have dreamed.

And it is well sometimes to leave our measuring line at home when we turn our thoughts to the church of Jesus Christ. There is a passion for statistics nowadays that can never without peril become dominant. I have a young friend who used to collect butterflies, and he was an adept at collecting butterflies. He would catch them with the deftest management and pin them down with a consummate artistry. And yet somehow they were never quite the same though catalogued with scientific accuracy; something of life had gone, something of sheen, something of the summer and the moor.

That is what always happens to the church when you try to catalogue it with scientific accuracy. Something of summer goes and of the moorland and of the wind that blows where it will, something of the poetry of Christ and of the high expectancy of miracle and of the power that falls from the very throne of God, and says, "Son of man, stand upon thy feet" (Ezek. 2:1). A church that you can put into a schedule is a church that you can put into an ashpit. To lose the immeasurable in the house of God is to lose everything that really matters. It is to lose the stirring of the heart. It is to lose the awaking of the conscience. It is to lose the quiet, ceaseless ministry of the living spirit of the Lord Jesus Christ.

I was down last week in one of our mission halls at a gathering of mothers there: three or four hundred poor and weary mothers were being helped and comforted and cheered. And I never saw any schedule from headquarters that had a separate column for that comforting. Yet in the sight of God and in the love of Christ, that is the only thing which really matters. It makes me angry with a righteous anger when I hear people sneering at the church. If they only knew what it was doing in Glasgow I do not think that they would sneer again—things so tender that you cannot tabulate them, things too beautiful even to be measured, things which not a hand in Glasgow does, save the delicate fingers of the bride of Christ. My critical brother, come and help the bride. She needs you, and she needs you sorely. It is better to be her friend and know her touch than to be the acutest critic in the world. To leave that measuring line at home a season and to begin to lend a hand in real earnest is the way to find that every Jerusalem is bigger and more glorious than you knew.

"A colt the foal of an ass" (Matt. 21:5).

12
The Message of the Colt *(A Palm Sunday Sermon)*

In the calendar of the Western Church today is the Sunday which is known as Palm Sunday. It is the Sunday preceding Easter Day which commemorates the triumphal entry into Jerusalem. Churches are decorated with palms today in remembrance of the waving of the palm branches. There are processions in Roman Catholic countries. And all this in memorial of that hour when our Savior took to Himself His royal state, and rode amid acclamations to His capital. Now in our Presbyterian Scotland we lay little stress upon these feasts and festivals. Even Christmas, the kindliest of them all, has only a partial and tardy recognition. Yet is there such a thing as common thought and the heightening of common life through common thought, and that is the spiritual value of such days. This evening, then, we shall join that strange procession moving across the valley to Jerusalem. We shall hear the shout that goes echoing down the glen, "Hosanna to the Son of David." We shall watch our Savior fulfilling ancient prophecy, proclaiming His mission as the prince of peace, riding on the colt into the city.

Now according to the narrative of Matthew there were two animals in that procession. There was an ass—a noble, honored beast—and then beside it there was the ass's colt. Both belonged to some one Jesus knew, probably to some one He had saved. Both were secured not far away from Bethany at a little hamlet called the House of Figs. And both were taken by the two disciples, and brought to the village for the Master's use and seemingly both were used in the procession. The point to note is this—according to all the gospels it was not upon the ass that Jesus mounted. He looked at both of them for one brief instant and then deliberately chose the colt. And in a life like His where everything is vital and the slightest action of a vast importance, reverent thought cannot ignore that choice. Can we in any measure understand it?

Well, to begin with, I suggest He made this choice as a *quiet assertion of His majesty*. He chose, and He quite deliberately chose, the animal on which man had never sat. That ass had long been used in burden-bearing. It had often carried its master to the market. It had borne his wife and children many a time when they went over the valley to the city. And it may be that when some temple doctor had lingered at Bethphage until the shadows fell, village kindness had conveyed him home mounted on that sleek and comely animal. For wife and children it was good enough. For priest or Pharisee nothing could be better. Even for Jesus, in His lowly ministry, it would have been a welcome ease in traveling. But now He was not Jesus but THE CHRIST. He was claiming for one brief hour His royal prerogative. He lifts Himself up into unique supremacy by choosing a beast whereon man had never sat. Long ago, down by the banks of Jordan, a very different scene had been enacted. With publicans and with soldiers and with sinners he had been baptized in the flowing Jordan. *There* He had stood where common men had stood. *Here* He sat where never man had sat. That both were quietly deliberate actions I see not how anyone can doubt.

For that, after all, is the abiding mystery of our Lord and Savior Jesus Christ. He was a man of sorrows and knew our human frailty, and yet He stands apart confronting us forever. No desperate sinner but knew Christ understood Him; no wearied woman but felt He was her friend; no innocent child but saw in those dear eyes something that witnessed to the thought of love. And yet with all that infinite compassion and understanding which never has been equaled, His soul was as a star and dwelt apart. He stood where sinful mortal man had stood, and yet He sat where never man had sat. He is nearer and dearer than the most loved brother, and yet He is mysterious and alone. He stands beside us, and yet He stands confronting us. He takes our hand, and yet He bows us down. For if Shakespeare came in tonight we should all stand, as Lamb[1] said; if He came in, we should all kneel. I do not think, then, that it was by accident that He chose the colt whereon man had never sat. Explain it how you will, *that* is the place which all the ages have given to Jesus Christ. And when you come to understand His power, to trust Him and in loyalty to follow Him, slowly and surely He will emerge for you into an incommunicable grandeur. Many a youth begins by putting Christ on the saddle where other men have sat. They put Him beside Socrates and Plato or give Him His place by Hegel and by Kant. And then the years go by, and troubles come, and no one can help and save but "Jesus only." He is on the colt whereon man had never sat.

In the second place, I would suggest to you that our Lord meant this choice *to typify His methods*. It was a quiet and a kindly parable of the kind of choices which He loves to make. As all of you are perfectly aware, in the Orient the ass was held in honor. It was a fine creature, says Professor David Smith, often as large as a small horse. Its bridle was studded with silver or with shells; its saddle was often elegant with tassels; it was associated in the people's thought with many a striking and historic scene. Now think of the striking contrast between that and the colt there by the ass's side: the one a trained and comfortable animal, the other a wild and shaggy little creature; the one accustomed to these crowded roads and going to take it easy whatsoever happened, the other rude and stubborn and intractable, filled with the fiery energy of youth. No hosannas would disturb the one; it was entirely safe and most entirely reputable.

But the other, never broken in as yet—no man could guarantee what it would do. And I think it was an acted parable, not without a certain courage in it, that our Lord rode that Sunday on the colt. Had He been thinking only of His comfort, our Lord would certainly have made the other choice. But I never read that in any choice He made our Lord thought of His safety or His comfort. It is not the first time, and it is not the last, that He has surprised the world by the servants He has chosen—the shaggy, fiery, and unbroken instruments for the advancement of His glory.

---

1. Charles Lamb (1775–1834), English poet and writer.

One would think, for instance, of the first disciples, and of what manner of instruments they were. One has only to read the record of the gospels to apprehend that they were coltish men. In Palestine in the period of our Savior, there was considerable culture of that kind.

There were men who were thoroughly trained and broken in by years of patient study of antiquity. There was a whole class known by the name of Pharisees, who walked in an odor of unquestioned sanctity and who stood in the eyes of all the common people for everything that was respectable and safe. The strange thing is that when Jesus made His choice, it was not any of such persons that He chose. He had no interest in *conventionality*; His only interest was in *possibility*. He did not want men who were broken *in*; He wanted men who were ready to break *out*, on a dead world that must be won for heaven and plucked even as a brand out of the burning.

That was why He chose these fiery natures, those untempered and unbroken men. Their ways were rude; their language was uncouth; their temper was uncertain and unproved. They were no sleek and comely beasts of burden, fitted to win applause in any pageant. They were rough colts, shaggy and undisciplined, yet chosen for the triumph of the Lord. It was a very daring choice to make. There were times when it actually seemed to be a failure. There were times when their stumbling and foolish obstinacy had almost broken the heart of the Redeemer. And I think that when He chose the colt that morning, instead of the sleek and comfortable creature, Peter and James and John would understand. They would feel that Christ had no misgivings. It would convey to them that He had no regrets. It would tell them that had He to choose again, His choice would not be made on different lines. And perhaps also it suggested to them that as they had shared His sufferings and sorrows, so would they share in the triumph that was coming when all the hosts of heaven would shout, "Hosanna!"

And if it was thus with the first chosen company, so has it been with every age since then. Not many wise, not many mighty, have been chosen to carry the Savior to His triumph. I am not one of those who think that Christ has any quarrel with learning or with literature. I believe that everything good and bright and beautiful is meant to be a handmaid in His kingdom. But I am one of those who, looking back on history and noting the hours when Christ has come in triumph, cannot but recognize in countless instances that He has ridden on the rude and shaggy colt. I think of the dignity of medieval Christendom, rent by the rude hand of Martin Luther. I think of an orthodox pulpit left unhonored, that the honor of service might be given to Bunyan. I think of an easy and comfortable England roused to a sense of God and of eternity, not by the fellows of any ancient college, but by an untrained creature like George Whitefield.

How often Christ has used the rugged word and left the most polished sermon ineffectual! How often has He owned the boisterous hymn and put to shame with it the praise of organs! How often has He come in power and triumph over the valley of our human need on the rough creature which was never trained and which no self-rejecting rabbi would have used. All that, to me, in kindly acted parable is typified in this action of Palm Sunday. It is Christ saying to us, "When you see this colt, you shall remember the Lord's ways until He come." And that is always needed by the Church when she waits for the ringing of the bridle-bells and thinks that Christ will never come to her, save on the sumptuous and splendid saddle.

I close by suggesting that this act of Palm Sunday may be rich in guidance and comfort for today. For as I look out on national life today, I see a cleavage which is ever deepening. I see on the one hand that world of precedent which we ennoble with the name of law and order. I see a world of immemorial usage, ancient right, and centuries of discipline. And I see another world of wild and turbulent forces, wakening into the consciousness of power, untrained in action because unused to action, untouched by the mellowing discipline of years. On the one hand the calm of ancient privilege and the quiet presumption of ancestral order. On the other hand rebellion and unrest, as of some wayward and unbroken beast. And hence the savage warfare of our day,[2] which needs no bloody wounds to make it real, whose chosen battlefields are our industrial centers and whose weapons are more deadly than the bayonet.

My fellow-citizen, it may be very terrible, but for the Christian it is thrilling as the dawn. We serve a Lord who chose the rudest and most undisciplined of creatures to carry Him. And so when I, a lover of things ancient, whose life is haunted by the

---

2. This sermon was preached before the outbreak of World War I.

storied past—when I am tempted to distrust the future and mourn the passing of an ancient order, I think of Him who on that Sunday morning chose the colt to bring Him to His triumph, a triumph that led by the bloody way of Calvary, to the joy of a new heaven and a new earth.

"Ye are come to an innumerable company of angels . . . and to Jesus" (Heb. 12:22, 24).

13
Angelic Ministry

"Do you believe in fairies, Mac?" asked Allan Cunningham[1] of a Celtic friend of his. "Indeed I'm not very sure," was the reply; "but do you believe in them yourself, Mr. Cunningham?"

"I once did," replied the burly poet, "and I would to God I did so still, for mountain and moor have lost much of their charm to me since my faith in their existence has departed." He then quoted Campbell's beautiful lines:

> When science from creation's face
> Enchantment's veil withdraws,
> What lovely visions yield their place
> To cold material laws.[2]

And so tonight if I were to ask, "Do you believe in angels?" I think there are some here who would give Allan Cunningham's reply. "I once did," you would say with a great wistfulness, "and I would to God I did so still." In the church in Thurso where I began my ministry we used to enter the pulpit through red curtains. And I

---

1. Allan Cunningham (1784–1842), Scottish poet and man of letters.
2. Thomas Campbell (1777–1844), patriotic Scottish poet.

often noticed a little child in front, gazing very intently at these curtains. She thought that behind these curtains there was heaven; she thought that the preacher came right out of heaven. Every time the curtains moved a little, she looked for the flashing of the wings of angels. Poor child! She has had many a sorrow since, and she has ceased to look for the angels long ago. She has learned that what she took for heaven once is only a dusty loft with spiders' webs in it. And if you asked her, "Do you believe in angels?" I dare say she might reply like Allan Cunningham, "I once did, and I would to God I did so still." Now we are all going to be children again tonight. For twenty minutes we shall believe in angels. We shall believe, as Jesus Christ believed, that in the heights of heaven there are angelic hosts. And then, taking the life of Jesus, we shall ask ourselves this simple question, "At what particular seasons in the life of Jesus do we discover the angels coming in?"

Well, in the first place, we light upon the angels in the season when our Lord was born. One of the most beautiful of all our Christmas carols is "Hark, the herald angels sing." Outwardly that birth at Bethlehem was an extremely insignificant event. Nobody wanted it—nobody heeded it—nobody thrilled that a great hour had come. Yet suddenly, in the dark midnight sky, there was an innumerable company of angels, singing, "Glory to God in the highest, good will toward men" (Luke 2:14). It tells us that things which seem of no account here may be of tremendous import in the sight of heaven. It tells us that all the depths of heaven may thrill with what the newspaper would never chronicle; tells us, and this is the great lesson, that though days may be coming which shall be dark with pain, the angels love to come at the beginning. It was a hard stern life that was in store for Christ. It was a life of battle and of storm. It was a life in which love was to prove recreant,[3] and the very kiss on the lips was to spell treachery. Yet at the very beginning of it all, and before the beauty of the dawn was on the mountains, suddenly there was *an innumerable company of angels*.

Do you smile at that? Do you think it a sweet fable? There is more truth sometimes in fables than in facts. When Christ was born there were angelic companies; there is that when everything beautiful is born. Here is a heart that has never known what love is, and

---

3. false

then in that dark manger love is born. And nobody heeds it in the clamorous streets more than they heeded the birth of Jesus Christ. And yet around that manger of the heart, where yesterday was the stir of common feet—today, an innumerable company of angels. The day is coming when love will have its cross, as the day was coming when Jesus had His cross. Shadows will fall, and money will be scanty, and little children will be very ill. But the life of love is like the life of Christ—it does not begin in shadow and in sorrow; it begins with the innumerable company of angels. Dreams that are golden—hopes that are ethereal—visions that are aglow with very heaven—voices that cry across the darkened plain "Glory to God, and on earth peace." It is to such music that all true love is born, nor do the echoes of it ever die away, even when the parched lips are on the sickbed or when the hungry wolf is at the door. Or think what happens when a high resolve is born. Have you ever had the courage to make a great decision? It is one of the joys of every fine decision that it puts an end to whispering human voices. Take your stand, and those who have enticed you shall move backward a little and leave room—room for an *innumerable company of angels.* To be weak is miserable, says Milton.[4] It is to be the sport of every passing breeze. But to make one fine resolve for Christ and courage is to draw to your side a thousand heavenly influences. It is to hear what you have never heard before and to see what you have never seen before in this mysterious universe of God. Days of dreary gloom are sure to follow, but no high passion ever begins in gloom. It is born in gladness and to the sound of music and with a vision of wings across an open heaven. And he who is wise will never forget that hour—which, valid once, is valid for eternity—when the mists come from the marshes by the sea.

I pass on to note, in the second place, that the angels came when Jesus was victorious. "Then the devil leaveth him, and, behold, angels came and ministered unto him" (Matt. 4:11). The gospel shows us in the clearest fashion the wiles of the devil in our Lord's temptation. Has it ever occurred to you as a very wonderful thing that we never read of any angels there? A legend would have had it full of angels; the heights of heaven would have been white with them, but there is nothing of all that in Scripture. Under a silent

---

4. John Milton (1608–1674), English poet.

heaven Christ fought His fight—out in a desert where He was alone. A single flash of an Ithuriel's[5] spear, and He would never have been tempted like as we are. Alone He stood—alone He fought His fight—alone with His own heart and God and Scripture. "Then the devil leaveth him, and, behold, angels came and ministered unto him." That is the second occasion on which the angels came, and the former was thirty years ago. They came when He was born and sang their music; *now*, when He is victorious. Not in the hour of wrestling with temptation, but when the devil is routed and the battle won, they appear again and minister to Him. How they ministered Scripture does not say. Perhaps they fed Him with the bread of angels. Perhaps they sang to Him such heavenly melody as made Him quite forget His gnawing hunger. But the point is that not when He was battling, but when He had stood and conquered in the battle, lo, an innumerable company of angels.

Now as it was with our Master in the desert, so is it with every one of us. The angels do not come when we are tempted; they come when we have crushed temptation under foot.

> Down to Gehenna and up to the throne,
> He travels the fastest who travels alone.[6]

There are hours when a man is terribly alone, and one is when he is fighting with the beast. But in the very moment that he conquers and says to the devil, "Get thee behind me, Satan" (Mark 8:33; Luke 4:8), in that very hour for him the heaven is radiant, and there is the sound of music in his ears. When a man has yielded where he should have resisted, when a man has fallen where he should have stood, you can tell by the very look upon his face that for him the daughters of music are brought low. But when a man in secret has fought his battle well, leaning upon the everlasting arm, the desert rejoices and blossoms as the rose. Common duties become nobler then. Common tasks take on a finer hue. The dullest day grows radiant as June if a man has fought the devil on that day. And to me that is the inward meaning of what I read in Scripture of the Lord, that when the devil leaves him, lo, an innumerable company of angels.

---

5. From Milton's "Paradise Lost."
6. From "The Winners" by Rudyard Kipling (1865–1936), English writer and poet.

And then, in the third place, I find the angel coming when the Lord was crucified and buried. They sang at Bethlehem—ministered in the desert—now they sit and watch within the tomb. According to one account there was *one* angel there, according to another there were *two*. Probably the sepulcher was full of angels, and men only saw what they had eyes to see. You go into a room that is quite full of people—so full that you have hardly room to move in it—and then you go out under the stars and say, "There was only one face in all that room for me."

Love has the clearest of all mortal vision, yet love can be magnificently blind. There may be fifty little children in the class, and to the mother there is only one. And so I like to think that in the sepulcher, as in the darksome heaven above Bethlehem, there was an innumerable company of angels. Now recall the hour when Jesus was betrayed; recall the words that He spoke to Simon Peter. Peter had plucked his sword out of its sheath and had cut off the ear of the High Priest's servant with it. And Jesus said to him, "Put up thy sword; dost thou think that I require thy puny arm? I can have legions of angels if I asked for them" (Matt. 26:52–53). The point to note is that He did not ask for them. The point to note is they were not given. In simple, loyal, childlike trust in God He faced the unutterable darkness of the cross. And then, when it was over and the end was come, and they took Him down and laid Him in the grave—suddenly an innumerable company of angels. To every human eye it looked like failure. In the eyes of heaven it did not look like failure. Heaven does not send its angels to ineptitude. It sends its angels to victorious issues. They had sung their music when He was born at Bethlehem. They had sung it when He triumphed in the wilderness. They sang it now when He lay within the grave.

And so I close with a word of cheer and comfort to all who have their cross to bear tonight. Explain it how you will, in this strange world the way of the cross is the way to angel-music. Every one of us has a cross to carry; the rich and the poor meet together there. O happy spirit—life of every company—tell me, have you not some cross to bear. We should never suspect it, meeting you in the street; you are so brave and bright and laughter-loving. But in every breast is the beating of a heart, and in every life the bearing of a cross. Now there are two things you can do with that cross of yours. There are two things, and there are only two. You can disown it—you can push it from you—or you can take it up and welcome it and carry it. And the singular thing is that when you do the former, invariably all the music ceases; but when you do the latter, lo, you are come to Jesus and to *an innumerable company of angels.*

"I found an altar with this inscription, TO THE UNKNOWN GOD" (Acts 17:23).

14
The Attraction of Agnosticism

Not very long ago in Glasgow there was a criminal trial which attracted much attention, not only by reason of its peculiar circumstances, but also because of certain observations of the judge. When the prisoner was being examined by counsel, one of the questions asked was, "Are you an atheist?" That was a very unusual question to be put in a modern court of law. No one, therefore, was very much surprised when Lord Guthrie, in giving the charge to the jury, dwelt with undisguised severity on that unusual interrogation. Now had the learned lord done nothing more than that, the aspect of things would have been entirely legal. But your true Scot is a theologian born—especially if he be born a Guthrie.[1] And so we had a little discourse on theology in which we were very wisely told that there are no atheists nowadays—only agnostics. I was struck by the very widespread notice which was given to that dictum of the judge. It found its way into all sorts of papers and was commented upon from every point of view. And so I have thought this might be a fitting time to say one or two words about agnosticism.

---

1. Thomas (Lord) Guthrie (1803–1873), philanthropist and organizer of the Free Church of Scotland.

Now I venture to think there are few here who do not know the meaning of these words. An atheist is one who denies that there is a God; an agnostic is one who denies that we can know God. The word agnostic is quite a modern word. It was coined, if I remember rightly, by Professor Huxley.[2] It was suggested by that verse in the Acts of the Apostles which tells of the altar raised to the unknown God. It is very significant that the view of things which utterly denies all revelation should have had to borrow its title from the Bible. An atheist has the courage of conviction. He lifts up his eyes and says there is no God. For him, heaven is a vacant place, and there is no eternal Personality. But the agnostic does not deny there is a God. All he asserts is that we cannot reach Him. He says that we are so constituted intellectually that to know God is utterly impossible.

You will observe that this agnostic attitude has nothing in common with Christian humility. It does not spring from the majesty of God, but from the limitations of our finitude. There are octaves of sound, in high and sunken registers, which no human ear is capable of hearing, yet to say that a thousand tones are imperceptible is not at all to say that man is deaf. And so the Christian reverently holds that there are heights and depths in God he cannot know, and yet he is convinced that God is knowable.

"Now we know in part and see in part" (1 Cor. 13:12); there is an agnosticism which is apostolic. There is a reverent veiling of our mortal gaze under the burning mystery of heaven. But to hold, as every Christian holds, that there are depths in God beyond our fathoming, is not to assert that God cannot be known. On the contrary, for the Christian consciousness, there is no such intense reality as God. He is nearer than breathing, closer than hands and feet, and more subtly present than any summer morning, evan though logic be powerless to reach and argument ineffectual to demonstrate Him, and life, in all the seeming tangle of it, too intricate a riddle to reveal Him.

"And when I saw him," says John, "I fell at his feet as dead" (Rev. 1:17); there were depths in the infinite which overwhelmed him. Yet that same John—with what triumphant certainty does he ring out the clarion cry, *We know*. And this is the glory of our Christian faith that,

---

2. Thomas Henry Huxley (1825–95), English biologist and early supporter of Darwin.

The Attraction of Agnosticism

with the fullest confession of great ignorance, it can yet lift up its voice out of the darkness and say, *I know whom I have believed.*

It is significant, let me say in passing, that the wheel of antagonism has now come full circle. This last subversal of the Christian faith is the intellectual negation of the first. When the new gospel was fighting for its life, it had one foe more deadly than all others. Some of you probably have never heard its name, though the later epistles are full of references to it. It was more deadly than any Jewish hatred. It was more subtle than any pagan ridicule. It wrought more havoc in the infant Church than the most cruel and bloody persecutions. Across the Empire from Ephesus to Lyons there was not a Christian community but suffered from it. It sapped the spiritual life of congregations and blighted the promise of countless catechumens. And this so subtle and insidious enemy, with which the infant Church fought for its life, was called by the forgotten name of *Gnosticism.* Now the word Gnostic, as students are aware, means exactly the opposite of Agnostic. The "Gnostic" is a man who says *I know*; the Agnostic is a man who says *I don't know.*

And the singular thing is that the Christian faith, which began by battling against a spurious knowledge, should now have to battle against a spurious ignorance. I regard this as a very hopeful sign for the ultimate triumph of the gospel. There is less hope for the man who says that he knows everything than for him who thinks that he knows nothing. For the one is unteachable, and in a world like this to be unteachable is to be condemned; the other has at least the aspect of humility. That is why in early Gnosticism the prevailing temper was one of scornful arrogance. And that is why in our modern Agnosticism we can so often detect a note of wistfulness. It is always a humbling thing to say, I do not know; doubly so to a keen and brilliant intellect; trebly so when the things it does not know are known to the humble crofter in the glen.

Indeed it is this last fact, when you consider it, that makes the attraction of Agnosticism so remarkable. It contradicts the deepest of all instincts, and yet it is acceptable today. That there is a God, and that that God is knowable, is the universal verdict of humanity. That there is a God, and that that God is knowable, is the instinct and affirmation of the soul. Yet when Agnosticism throws out its challenge and repudiates these universal witnesses, it finds a welcome in the modern mind. That is a very remarkable phenomenon, well worthy of our consideration. At Gnosticism we all smile today, but at Agnosticism no one thinks to smile. And what I suggest is that this is only explicable on the ground of a certain specious affinity between the negative creed of the agnostic and the general spirit of the age. Professor Lecky[3] has taken pains to show that it is not argument which kills beliefs. It is rather those slow and subtle changes which gradually permeate the spirit of a people. But not only do these slow and subtle changes explain the destruction of ancient superstition; they explain also the emergence of beliefs. Every creed demands its fit environment as absolutely as does the Alpine flower. Without that environment it will never flourish though it be preached with genius and passion. And I want to show you how the agnostic creed, which once would have been treated with derision, has found a fitting environment today.

Agnosticism, for instance, seems to answer readily to our altered thought of the dwelling place of man. "What is man, that thou art mindful of him" (Ps. 8:4) has meaning for us the psalmist never knew. So long as man deemed that the world which he inhabited was the great and glorious center of the universe, for so long was it natural for him to hold that he was important in the eyes of heaven. But if his dwelling-place be but an atom, flying through boundless space where worlds are numberless, then things assume a different complexion. Now that is exactly what modern science has done. It has dislodged our world from its centrality. It has robbed us of our cosmic importance and made us the creatures of a tiny planet. And it was inevitable that this altered thought, which has so profoundly influenced man's attitude to nature, should have influenced also his attitude to God.

It was natural to believe that God was knowable when just beyond the clouds He had His throne. But heaven has gone very far away now, and we sweep the depths of space and cannot find it. And so having learned on evidence unquestioned, the actual insignificance of earth, we begin to doubt the significance of man. It is to that temper Agnosticism comes. It is the creed which answers that suspicion. It is not presumptuous as was atheism. It does not dare to say there is no God. It only says that for creatures such as we are, fashioned of the dust of a little distant planet, the proper attitude is one of ignorance.

---

3. William Lecky (1838–1903), British historian.

The Attraction of Agnosticism

But if men would only think a little, they would see the fallacy of that appeal. There is a little cottage down in Ayrshire to which pilgrims turn with tender hearts. It has no grandeur as of marble staircase nor spacious rooms with decorated ceiling. Yet he who was born there would have been no greater had he been cradled in a kingly palace, nor was he less a genius because a cottage-child. It is not the dwelling-place that makes the man; it is the man that makes the dwelling place. There may be depths of meanness in the lordliest home and moral grandeur in the poorest dwelling. And to argue that man must be a cipher because the world is not a lordly dwelling-place is like arguing that Burns[4] was not a genius because he was a cottage-child. On the contrary, it seems to me that the evidence is the other way. For it is not in palaces nor lordly manors that moral and spiritual worth is most often found. It is in humble homes with lowly roofs, which have no beauty that we should desire them and which never obtrude themselves upon the passerby. Search through Scotland for the men who know, and you will not find them in the grandest dwellings. It is not in the castles of Dumbartonshire that you find the students who know Shakespeare. And so to argue that God cannot be known, unless the world be the castle of the universe, is to move contrary to all experience.

But there is another attraction of Agnosticism which helps to explain its prevalence today. It is in apparent harmony with an age that cannot brook the accent of finality. To say *I do not know* is not dogmatic, at least it does not seem to be dogmatic, and so it answers to that prevailing spirit which cannot tolerate the thought of dogmatism. Probably we are suffering today for the over-dogmatism of the past. You will very generally find an age of doubt after an age of overconfident assertion. And it may be that the preaching of a former generation, which was so absolutely confident of everything, has given us an age which is confident of nothing. Whatever the cause be, this at least is plain, that men today are not in love with dogmatism. They may have a wistful yearning for the Christ, but they are easily irritated at the creed. They do not accept the sufficiency of formulas. They are no longer held by orthodox beliefs. They are impatient at the suggestion of finality.

That there is a nobler side to this impatience, I think it is only fair

---

4. Robert Burns (1759–96), Scottish poet.

to recognize. It is always the characteristic of an age that is trembling on the verge of discoveries. And that we are now trembling on the verge of such discoveries as will revolutionize our life and thought, I have not the shadow of a doubt. Now whenever there is such expectancy abroad, the one intolerable standpoint is finality. To be dogmatic in a world of mystery is to seel[5] the eye so that it cannot see. And any creed which cuts as with a saber into the heart of all dogmatic doctrine is certain to receive a kindly welcome. There have been ages when a teacher had no audience unless he could lift up his voice and say *I know*. But today a far more powerful appeal is to lift up the voice and say *I do not know*. And that is the attraction of Agnosticism to an age that is a little weary of dogmatics and is beginning to feel again in countless ways the wonder and the mystery of things.

But the curious thing is that Agnosticism has proved itself the most intolerant of dogmatisms. Professing to be the foe of all finality, it is itself the most final of all creeds. Through all the ages the gospel has maintained itself with an infinite and living power of adaptation. It has responded to all the growth of knowledge and never forfeited its central verities. But Agnosticism in these past forty years—and what are forty years to twenty centuries—has only saved itself from utter ruin by the very dogmatism which it scorns. To say we have no evidence for God may sound like intellectual humility. It may seem to indicate a very different temper from the blatant atheism of fifty years ago. But when you are dealing not with things but with *persons*, to say that you have no proof of their existence is really to deny that they exist.

There might be gold under the snows of Greenland though we had no evidence that gold was there. But if there were little children in a home, would they not be certain to betray their presence? And if you found no nursery nor cot, nor picture books, nor fragmentary toys, would not that mean there were no children there? That would be the verdict of the briefest visit; but what if you lived for years within the dwelling? What if you lived there day and night for years and never

---

5. Author's Note: In justice to my most excellent printers may I point out that this is not a misprint for seal. That fine old expression "to seel up the eyes" has nothing to do with sealing (L. *sigillum*), it is the O. F. *siller les yeux*, fr. L. *cilium*.

Mine eyes no more on vanitie shall feed,
But seeled up with death, shall have their deadly meed.

The Attraction of Agnosticism

found one proof that there were children? You see in a moment that to find no evidence is to be driven to deny their being; and as with little children, so with God. If even a shipwrecked sailor on an island leaves unmistakable traces of his presence, how much more the Creator of the universe!

Now that is where Agnosticism fails. It has never been able to maintain itself. It has not been able, like the faith of Christ, to stand foursquare to every wind that blew. It has either gravitated far nearer atheism than Lord Guthrie would allow us to admit, or it has crept back to the feet of God again. I confess I have no faith in any creed that cannot maintain itself for forty years. I have a strong suspicion that the truth must lie with one that has stood the storm and shock of centuries. And when I find it meeting my deepest need and answering the crying of my heart, by it I am content to live and die. For character is not built upon negations, nor does life come to its victories that way. Life is too difficult and dark and terrible to be fought out by what I do not know. It is when I can say after the strain of years, *I know whom I have believed* (2 Tim. 1:12), that my feet are planted on the rock.

"We shall see him as he is" (1 John 3:2).

15
The Crowning Vision

Whether we shall see *God* as He is, is a question that has been often agitated in the schools. No man has seen God at any time (John 1:18). That we shall know Him with a knowledge intimate and satisfying is the scriptural hope which we all cherish. God so interpenetrates all heaven that to be in heaven is to be in God. But whether we shall see Him face to face and have an immediate vision of His being is a question on which men have reverently differed. Even the seraphim around the throne veil their faces with their wings before Him. These mighty creatures, the bodyguard of heaven, cannot brook the glory of the Lord. And so it has been reverently questioned whether it will ever be possible for mankind to see a glory which they cannot bear.

But if God, in His essential being, may be forever shrouded from our human gaze, it is not so with the Lord Jesus Christ. If there is one thing clear upon the page of Scripture, it is that when the believer wakes in glory he shall behold his Savior face to face. Now we see through a glass darkly (1 Cor. 13:12); we are like men beholding in a mirror. We walk by faith, or we strive to walk by faith, and faith is the evidence of things not seen (Heb. 11:1). But when earth retires and we awake in heaven, faith shall be perfected in sight; and then we shall see Him as He is. Eye has not seen and

The Crowning Vision

ear has never heard the things that God has prepared for them that love Him (1 Cor. 2:9). That is the faith in which the saints have lived, and it is in such a faith that they have died. And of all the things that God has so prepared there shall be nothing half so wonderful or satisfying as the immediate vision of our Savior.

I should like to say in passing that these words of John are to be taken in their deepest sense. We shall see Him as *He is*. Our first thought would be to take these words as a vivid contrast to what our Savior *was*. Now we see Him as He was; then we shall see Him as He is. But the thought of the apostle goes far deeper than any difference between past and present; we are to see Him as He really is. John knew, as all the apostles knew, that his exalted Lord was always one. That He is the same yesterday and forever is the consistent testimony of the apostles. And what John means is that now we see Him dimly, whether in Galilee or on the throne, but then we shall see Him as He is. In our very clearest moments here we see Christ but dimly and imperfectly. All we have ever seen and known of Him is, as it were, "the outskirts of his ways." And the wonder of the sight of heaven is this, that with eyes made perfect by the love of God, for the first time we shall see Him as He is.

It is often a very thrilling moment when we first see people as they really are. We thought we knew them, and then some hour arrives when heights and depths in them flash out upon us. And then we feel that we have never known them, never understood their real character, never fathomed their depths of personality. In some such way, when we awake in heaven, we shall feel that we have never known the Savior. Now we know in part and see in part; then shall we know even as we are known. At last, when we are purged and purified, and when the love of God has given us eyes to see, we shall see Him as He is.

It is this immediate vision of the Lord which will crown the blessedness of heaven. The joy of heaven is the beatific vision. That heaven is a very real place is the unvarying teaching of the Bible. "I go to prepare a place for you," says Christ, and "in my Father's house are many mansions" (John 14:2). But a mansion may be very beautiful and adorned with every treasure wealth can purchase, and yet the heart may be very lonely there. There is nothing more desolate than a great home when somebody who was its light is gone. All that art can minister and wealth supply seems but a mockery in such an hour. And so the very magnificence of heaven would only make it a more lonely place if the presence of our Savior were not there. As with homes, so is it too with countries, and heaven is often spoken of as a country. The most beautiful scenery God ever made can never satisfy the human heart. And heaven shall be far more beautiful than earth, for it is reality and earth the shadow, and yet a man might be unhappy in it. That is why Paul, whenever he thinks of heaven, immediately passes to the thought of Christ. He knew all about the sea of glass, but he never dwells on that. He never says, when life is hard and difficult, "I have a desire to depart and go to heaven"; he says, "I have a desire to depart, and be *with Christ*" (Phil. 1:23).

That we shall see Him there as He is we may regard as certain, when we remember that there we shall see Him *at home*. I think you must always see a man at home if you want to see him as he really is. Of course, there are some homes of which that is not true. There are homes where a person is not his real self. That is especially true of sensitive children in homes where there is more ridicule than sympathy. And the untold evil of such homes is this, that they make the child shrink into himself, which is the very thing God meant no child to do. It has not been my lot to meet with many hypocrites, but I have watched them closely whenever I have met them. My experience is that very often hypocrisy can be traced back to the home. When a child is repressed instead of being encouraged, when it is afraid to open its lips lest it be jeered at, then it grows reticent and loses all self-confidence, and hypocrisy becomes perilously easy.

But while that is true and very sadly true, it only emphasizes what I have been saying, that where there is love and sympathy at home, it is there that a man is seen just as he is. He may be a better man or he may be a worse man than he is in the judgment of the world. He may be far more generous, amiable, patient; or, on the other hand, he may be less so. But the point is that in the freedom of the home, where there is love and fellowship and sympathy, a man is recognized in his true nature. I have been honored by the friendship of good men whose names are fragrant in city and in market, men whom the bitterest rival never dared to associate with a dishonorable thing; yet there were depths in them of patient love and heights of idealism quietly realized, that could never be known to anyone on earth save to those who had the friendship of their homes.

The Crowning Vision

And there "we shall see him as he is"; in heaven we shall see Him in His home. We shall no longer see Him among those who scorn Him; we shall see Him among the multitudes who love Him. Foxes have holes and the birds of the air have nests, but the Son of Man has no place to lay His head (Matt. 8:20; Luke 9:58). He had only one place here to lay His head, and that was on the cross. And if here, despised and rejected, He was so wonderful and full of grace—what will He be at home! Here He could not turn but men were watching Him. Here He was always being misinterpreted. Here, when He wanted to do a deed of love, they laughed Him to scorn. And if in spite of all that human treatment He was so gloriously and infinitely gracious here, what will He be in the liberty of home? There will be nobody to insult Him there. There will be none to hinder Him because of unbelief. Love will surround Him, and nothing else than love, in the multitude whom He has ransomed. And who can tell what depths will be disclosed then in Him who was so exquisitely gracious when He on earth could not move a finger without cavil.[1]

Then, once again, we shall see Him as He is because we *shall be no longer children*. "Beloved, now are we the children of God; but it doth not yet appear what we shall be" (1 John 3:2). In our version it is translated "sons of God," but in the revised version you will find it *children*. That is a small change but a very important one, and what it means is this. It means that the word for "sons" (which Paul was so fond of) is a different word from the one which John here uses, and it is different because the thought is different. When Paul speaks of the sons of God, he thinks of the liberties of sonship. But when John speaks of the children of God, he thinks of the weakness and ignorance of childhood.

And so John says, "Beloved, we are children now—ignorant and inexperienced children—but the day is coming when we shall not be children, and then we shall see him as he is." Many of you here this evening can appreciate that out of your own experience. When you were a child, let me say, you had a loving father, and even as a child you knew he loved you. But it was not until you grew to manhood or to womanhood, perhaps when your father was sleeping in his grave, that you ever really understood his character. As a child you used to see him writing or going out in the evenings. Or perhaps some evening

---

1. frivolous or trivial opposition

he would be very quiet, and your mother would watch him with an anxious face. But what it all might mean you did not know then, because you were children at the time. My friend, you know it all today. You know how honored and loved your father was. You are no longer children, and so now you see what as a child you had no eyes to see. And beloved, now are we God's children, and it has not yet been manifested what we shall be, but we know that when it shall be manifested, we shall see Him as *He is*. Every believer shall be a son in heaven, but no believer will be a child in heaven. The love of God will draw us into adult life, fresh from the releasing of the grave. In that adult life we shall begin to see what here as children we have no eyes to see, the wonder of the love of Jesus Christ. Words will come back to us we heard in childhood and which we never understood in childhood. Things that seemed cruel and hard to us in childhood will dawn upon our memories again. And being no longer children but grownups under the quickening of the love of God, we shall understand at last what it all meant. "When I was a child, I spake as a child, I understood as a child, I thought as a child. But when I became a man, I put away childish things" (1 Cor. 13:11). And so in heaven, being no longer children, we shall put away our childish ignorance and at last shall see Him as He is.

The third ground of our assurance that we shall see Him so, lies in the fact that then *we shall be like Him*. "We know that when he shall appear we shall be like him," and being like Him, "shall see him as he is." Unless you have some affinity with people, you never see them as they really are. You must have the music of poetry within you if you are really to understand a poet. Personality is wonderfully sensitive—not consciously but by its very nature—and never reveals itself in any fullness save under the sunshine of affinity. You may have known a man for years, yet never known him, just because you are radically different from him. And then someone comes along who understands him by some divine affinity of nature. And in a week or two that kindred soul begins to see what you have never seen; he is like him and sees him as he is. That is especially the case with children. They have an unerring instinct for those who understand them. You must have the childlike heart to see the child. You must have the Christlike heart to see the Savior. And it is just because at last we shall be like Him, in the fullness of our glorified humanity, that in heaven we shall see Him as He is.

"And we have seen and do testify that the Father hath sent the Son to be the Savior of the world" (1 John 4:14).

16
Christ and the Home
(A Christmas Meditation)

There are two thoughts which meet and mingle when we gather together at a Christmas season. The one is the thought of Jesus Christ, and the other is the thought of home. The very name that we give to this happy time has Christ for its first and most important syllable—this is not Candlemas nor Marymas; this is *Christ*mas. And then the manger and the swaddling clothes and the newborn infant and the mother, all these speak to us of home. We have seasons when we associate Christ with heaven; we have Easter Sunday and Whitsunday.[1] But at Christmas—though it be full of heaven—it is natural to associate Christ with home. And so tonight we shall think of Christ a little in his connection with the life of home, the sweetest and tenderest of all relationships.

How deeply Christ had been influenced by His home is apparent to every reader of the gospels. Through all His life and ministry and death, the music of home rings like a sweet refrain. As life goes on, and the years unfold their chronicle, we all discover that home has been determinative. We never escape it. It is always with us. It tells

---

1. Seventh Sunday and fiftieth day after Easter celebrating Pentecost.

to our dying hour in weal or woe. That is why every biography begins, not with the hour of effort or achievement, but with the father's stock, and with the mother's ancestry, and with the environment of infant days. A man may travel to the far Antipodes, or he may rise to be the friend of princes; there are two things which he never leaves behind when he takes the wings of the morning or mounts with wings as eagles. One is the fore-ordering will of God, who sees the end from the beginning, and the other is the influence of home. Like a sweet fragrance or a cloudy vapor it clings to his garments until his dying hour. Like some fine tonic or some insidious poison it courses in his blood with every heartbeat. And therefore the irreparable loss in life when homes are foolish, worldly, uninspiring, when motherhood suggests no lovely things, when fatherhood recalls no comradeship.

This influence of home, felt by us all, was felt in its full intensity by Christ. In His words and deeds—in His life and in His death—"home sweet home" is like a sweet refrain. The first miracle He ever wrought was performed in a home and at a marriage feast. The most beautiful parable He ever uttered was about a son who was a prodigal. The richest and deepest name He had for God was drawn from the tender relationships of home—"Our *Father* which art in heaven" (Matt. 6:9). This man spoke as never man spoke. He spoke as many of us would be ashamed to speak. We speak of tendencies and of environment. He spoke of little children in the marketplace. He spoke of a woman sweeping out a cottage, of another baking in the kitchen, and of a father who was brokenhearted as he thought of a prodigal son in a far country. Like a great wave the thought of home broke over Him when He saw a widow mourning for her child. He called to His aid the mighty power of heaven just to give her back her son again.

And all this shows that in the thought of Christ such simple words as son and child and mother were infinitely precious and important. Somehow or other, then, right through the life of Jesus you feel the power and influence of home. It colors His language. It inspires His miracles. It kindles His passion and directs His vision. Even amid the agonies of Calvary and in the hour of excruciating pain, the old familiar music is not silent.

Well now, I want you to think tonight where that melody of home was born. It was not born in the high expanse of heaven. It was born in the lowly home at Nazareth. There are men and women whom we sometimes meet who irresistibly suggest to us that their home was beautiful. There is a touch which nothing else can give that tells of a beautiful and reverential childhood. And that man must be blind as any Cyclops after Odysseus[2] had wrought his havoc, who does not recognize that touch in Christ. We talk of the silent years at Nazareth. They are only silent because we make them so. There is music enough and to spare waiting to fill them, out of the oratorio that follows. The evangelists were too wise to go to Nazareth to interrogate some patriarchal villager; they said, Do you want to know about Christ's home? Study His ministry and find it there. What could the gossips in Nazareth have known? The best and most beautiful homes have no history. It is when homes are unhappy and when parents quarrel that the neighbors are able to satisfy the chronicler. The most beautiful homes are always quiet homes and leave no record in any village gossip. Their only record is the children's lives, when duty calls and when the battle comes. We talk and sing of the fair green hills of Nazareth, and I have no doubt these hills were very fair. But judging by the years which are preserved for us, there was one thing at Nazareth fairer still to Christ. It was the home where as a boy He played, watched His mother tidying and baking, and heard her singing, when the day was over, of "old unhappy far-off things."[3]

One would observe in passing that from the gospel record it is clear that Christ was never ashamed of home. There are sons and daughters who are ashamed of home and of their fathers and their mothers also. It was a very old-fashioned home, that home at Nazareth. It was a home of sweet and simple piety. It had caught no polish from the Roman empire; Joseph was but a humble working man. It was a home like countless homes in Scotland, whose only adornment is the fear of God but which have sent out sons to teach and preach and heal or to govern the millions of India. It is not such sons who are ever ashamed of home. They honor their father and their mother. They come back to the cottage from their Indian palace and are proud to call that bent old woman *mother*. The kind of

---

2. From the *Odyssey*, attributed to Homer (850 B.C. ?).
3. From "The Solitary Reaper" by William Wordsworth (1770–1850), English poet.

children who are ashamed of home and of a father who has never learned his manners are the children whose infinitely little world is their infinitely little selves. Think of it, friends, Christ was the King of kings, and yet He never was ashamed of Nazareth; never despised it—never once ignored it—never blushed at being the carpenter's son. And if ever you have been tempted so—and I know not how you have been tempted—I want you to put it right this Christmas Sunday.

It is clear also from the gospel narrative that Christ knew the temptations of the home. The words of Christ that have the harshest ring in them are the words He spoke to those who loved Him most. To the sinner Christ was infinitely pitiful. A bruised reed He would not break (Isa. 42:3). Even with Judas there is the note of gentleness: "Friend, wherefore art thou come?" (Matt. 26:50). But sometimes in the hour of fierce temptation there is a violent recoil that looks like harshness, and that is only found with those who loved Him.

There was one who loved Him more than any other. It was the mother who had cradled Him. With all the wonderful tenderness of motherhood she clung in yearning love to her firstborn. And when the spirit of God came down on Him at Jordan, and He was driven from home into the wilderness, it was like a dagger in His mother's heart. The eternal mystery of love is this, that it holds within its breast a twofold craving—the craving to give and to give everything, and also the quenchless craving to possess. You have them both in the perfect love of God, which gives to the uttermost, yet wants us always; you have them both in the mother-love of Mary. She could not release her hold upon her child. She wanted Him and wanted Him at home. It was breaking her heart that He should run such risks and fling a defiance that must end in death. And so she sought Him, tried to interfere with Him, and wanted Him back in the quiet peace of Nazareth, and to Christ that was a terrible temptation.

The worst temptations do not come from enemies—the worst temptations come from those who love us, from those who would lay their lives down for us gladly and yet have never heard our calling voices, from those to whom we have to say sometimes, as the poet said on going to the wars, "I could not love thee, dear, so much, loved I not honor more."[4] There comes a time in many a

---

4. From "To Lucasta, Going to the Wars" by Richard Lovelace (1618–58) English poet.

person's life when the thought of home must take a second place. Visions are beckoning—there is the call of God—conscience is crying and will not be denied. And there can be no question that our blessed Lord felt that temptation in its full intensity, for He was tempted in all points like as we are (Heb. 4:15). When you are tempted in such ways as that, remember that Jesus understands when you are tempted by dear human love to be a traitor to the call of God. It is Nazareth and the love of Mary which gives their infinite pathos to these words, "Whoso loveth father or mother more than me is not worthy of me" (Matt. 3:37).

There was one trial at home which Jesus knew, and which it is well we too should remember. He not only knew what it was to be loved at home, but He knew what it was to be misunderstood at home. There was a period in the life of Principal Rainy[5] when he was exposed to violent abuse. Hardly a day passed but in the newspapers his actions were misrepresented and distorted. And one day, in Melville Street in Edinburgh, Dr. Whyte[6] met him. "Rainy," he said, "I can't understand you, you seem as radiant and blissful as a child." And Dr. Rainy answered very quietly, "Ah, but Whyte, *I'm very happy at home.*"

When a man is happy at home, he can face anything. Even the newspaper holds no terrors. It is not the misunderstanding of the public that weighs a straw with men whose hearts are pure. But one of the sorest trials of human life, especially where life is young and ardent, is to be misunderstood *at home*. To get no sympathy within the home—to have no one there who really understands—to find all natural utterance repressed—to hear the cherished ideal being sneered at, for sensitive impressionable youth there are few things harder in life to bear than that, and such was the experience of Jesus.

Many believed in Him—let us be thankful. But none of His brothers, we are told, believed in Him. Like Joseph's brethren, when he came home at night they would say, "Behold, this dreamer cometh" (Gen. 37:19). And how that must have weighed upon the

---

5. Robert Rainy (1826–1906), professor of Church History, New College, Edinburgh.

6. Alexander Whyte (1837–1921), minister of the Free Church of Scotland and author.

Lord in the eager delicate beauty of His youth, I leave with you to try to realize.

Do I speak to any who are all alone at home? Who find no sympathy from brother or from sister? To any who would never dream of uttering at home all that is deepest in their hearts, my lonely hearer, in the home at Nazareth and right on to the hour of resurrection, remember that our Lord had that to bear.

I close by suggesting to you another thought, that Jesus bore the *burden* of the home. For it is commonly held, and held, I think, with truth, that Joseph died while our Lord was still in boyhood. The last time we hear of Joseph is when the family went up to Jerusalem together. After that we always hear of Mary; after that we never hear of Joseph. Just when the crisis of the child had come, just when He heard the calling of the world, He had to go home again, and take the burden up, and support the household as a carpenter.

"Wist ye not I must be about my Father's business?" (Luke 2:49). That tells you what was surging in His heart. He had been dreaming of kingdoms in these quiet days, or the devil would never have tempted Him with kingdoms. Then Joseph died, Mary was a widow, and the younger children must have bread to eat—and the Lord became the carpenter of Nazareth. For long years out of the thirty-three, King of kings and Carpenter of Nazareth! And no one knew in all that sleepy hollow what dreams and hopes were burning in His heart—but the devil knew when he tempted Him with kingdoms. I beg of you not to call them silent years. To me they are most eloquent and vocal. They are filled with the heroism of quiet duty. They are sublimely faithful in the least. And if you are looking for a happy Christmas and still more for a radiant New Year, remember that, and with new faith and loyalty turn to your lowly task again.

"Take heed what ye hear" (Mark 4:24).

17
The Responsibility of Hearing

On the responsibility attaching to our *speaking,* our Lord was never weary of insisting. He has given a significance to human words which has altered their character forever. These syllables, invisible as air, are indestructible as adamant. They are the opposite of the snowflake on the river, which is "a moment white, then gone forever."[1] According to the consistent teaching of our Lord, our words are shaping our eternal destiny, and by them as by the flower of the life, we shall be judged.

But if our Lord insists, as He does constantly, upon the responsibilities of speaking, we must never forget that with an equal emphasis He insists on the responsibilities of *hearing.* Often when He was beginning a discourse and sometimes when He was concluding a discourse, He would pause a moment and look around the company, and say, "He that hath ears to hear, let him hear." It was a solemn summons to reflection, flung out upon a crowd who were all listening—a sharp and swift reminder to His audience of the responsibility attaching to all hearing. There was a sense in which all heard alike, for when Jesus spoke, He lifted up His voice. Some carry the cross of ineffectual voices, but I do not imagine it was so

---

1. From "Tam o' Shanter," by Robert Burns (1791).

with Him. But there was another sense in which every man who listened heard something a little different from his neighbor, and Christ was intensely aware of that divergence. "He that hath ears to hear, *let him hear*." All were listening, yet not all were hearing. Christ knew it intuitively and sympathetically. He read it in the look upon their faces. And so do we learn that He who felt intensely the responsibility which clings to speaking, felt, and often gave expression to, the responsibility which is attached to hearing.

In the parallel passage of St. Luke our text assumes a slightly different form. It is softened and toned down a little and becomes, Take heed *how* ye hear. Such an injunction as that is not arresting; it would not touch nor startle anybody. Every Galilean schoolboy knew that if he was half asleep in school, he would be punished. What Jesus actually said was far more penetrating and would send listeners home to ponder and reflect; not take heed how ye hear, but take heed *what* ye hear. It is commonly held, and I think rightly held, that Peter dictated these logia[2] to Mark. And I can fancy Mark suggesting a mistake here, for Mark was young enough to be omniscient. And then I can picture the veteran apostle, who had done forever with betraying Christ, bidding his amanuensis[3] hold his tongue and write exactly as he bade him do. Christ was fond of saying startling things, and this is one of His most startling things. Take heed *how* ye hear is commonplace; take heed *what* ye hear is revelation. For it tells us that in the kind of things we hear there is more than the impact of the wave of air. There is our love and hate. There is our ruling passion. There is character and destiny.

Of course there is a large and literal sense in which hearing is independent of the will. And of course our Savior knew that perfectly, for He was always in living touch with fact. No man can choose entirely what he hears, any more than he can choose entirely what he sees. There is an element of necessity in life. It is the ground on which our liberty is built. Every day there are ten thousand sounds traveling toward us in unseen vibration, and just because God has made the ear to hear, we hear them whether we will or no. He whose lot is cast in the great city cannot be deaf to the uproar of the street. He whose home is on the edge of the

---

2. sayings of a religious teacher, especially Jesus
3. secretary

ocean cannot escape the music of the sea. In the physical impact of all sound there is a region where the will is powerless, and Jesus was perfectly aware of that. The point is that when Jesus spoke of hearing, it was not of the physical impact that He thought. For Him no sound had traveled all its course until it had reached from the ear into the soul. And it is when the soul in its inherent liberty passes its inevitable verdict, that the thing we hear becomes a moral thing, carrying an infinite significance. "Two men looked out of the prison bars. The one saw mud, the other stars"[4] It was the same prospect that they looked upon, and yet to hope and to despair—how different! And so to different ears come the same words, identical in cadence and in syllable, and yet how diverse their interpretation in the selective power of the soul. It is not really by the eye we see. It is really by the *soul* we see. And it is not by the ear we hear. It is indeed by the character we hear. By all we love, by all we have made ourselves, by all we have striven for or lusted after, do we take the words which fall on every ear and color them with heaven or with hell. Take heed what you hear, my friend. It is a revelation of your personality. It is in the verdicts which you are always passing that your responsibility begins. Every sermon worth a scrap is a revelation of the preacher, but remember that in the thought of Christ it is also a revelation of the hearer.

In one of the lessons which we read this evening that thought is very significantly illustrated. I refer to the lesson from the Gospel of St. John, where we read of the visit of the Greeks to Christ. "Father, glorify thy name," said Jesus, and then there came an answering voice from heaven (John 12:28). And Jesus and the disciples heard it, and all the company who were standing around; when they heard it, some said it thundered, and others that an angel spoke to Him. Think of it, it was the voice of God: the audible utterance of the Creator. And it fell alike on every listening ear of the men and women who were gathered there. And yet for some of them there was no more in that than the distant roll of thunder in the hills; for others there was the music of the angels. Each caught the selfsame utterance of heav-

---

4. Frederick Langbridge (1849–1923), "A Cluster of Quiet Thoughts" (1896):
"Two men look out through the same bars:
One sees the mud, and one the stars."

en. Each heard what he had trained himself to hear. It was the same accent upon every ear but a different accent within every soul. And that is what Jesus means when He enjoins us to take heed *what* we hear, for what we hear betrays the personality.

One might illustrate that in many ways. We might think, for instance, of the home. We might think of those childish stammerings of speech that succeed the "only language" of a cry. Those broken syllables—those childish lispings—those faint irrecognizable resemblances—how little these convey of any value to the indifferent or uninterested heart. But to the mother they are full of meaning, and she is never weary listening to them; to her they are the sweetest music in the world. She does not hear them with a fleshly ear. She hears them with a mother's heart. She brings that gift of heaven, a mother's love, to the interpreting of every syllable. And so by what she hears she trains her child, yet in so doing she reveals herself and stands before us self-confessed in motherhood. Love a person, and his speech is sweet. Hate him, and his every word is barbed. It is by love and hate and jealousy and envy that we record and register the utterance. And thus is it always vital to self-knowledge not only to take heed to what we say, but also to take heed to what we *hear*.

That strange divergence of the recording faculty has in our modern life one notable expression. It is the bane, perhaps it is the necessity, of the development of party-politics. With party-politics as party-politics the Christian minister has no concern. But with the temper fostered by such politics the Christian minister has every concern. And there is certainly no sphere in modern life which more powerfully or constantly exemplifies that there is no such thing in the affairs of men as what may be called neutrality of hearing. Some great statesman makes a speech, and the news of it is flashed along the wires. And the next day in a hundred newspapers it stands precisely as it was delivered. And to one man it is the voice of angels and thrilling as with the music of a trumpet; to another, hearing the selfsame words, it is sound and fury signifying nothing. Nothing is registered on a clean slate. There is no such thing in life as a clean slate. Nothing falls upon a virgin ear. There is no such gateway to the soul. Men hear by every ideal that they cherish—by every battle they have lost or won—by every ancient privilege they guard—by every dream that they have ever dreamed. All our hope is in our hearing, and all our selfishness is in our hearing. All the right that we have ever sought, and all the wrong that we have ever

The Responsibilty of Hearing

done. That is the response of human character to everything that falls upon the ear, and our response is our responsibility.

The same thing is always happening in the hearing of the gospel message. A hearer's judgment of a gospel sermon is really the judgment of himself. With patient and with prayerful diligence a minister prepares his message. He has his ideals of what preaching is, and from those ideals nothing will make him swerve. And then, often in fear and trembling, and sometimes with a joyous sense of liberty, he gives his message to his beloved people. It is the same message which falls on every ear, and yet how different is the response! It is the same tidings of the grace of God, and yet how varying is the reception! All that is living in the hearer's breast rises up to meet a living message and rises in welcome or defiance. Men hear with all that they have made themselves. They hear with every sin to which they are clinging. Every ambition, every joy or sorrow, comes to the hearing of a gospel sermon. And that is why to one it shall be weariness, and to another a thing to be disproved, and to a third, in hungriness of heart, the message shall be the very bread of angels. It is a great responsibility to preach. It is a great responsibility to hear. I know no teacher except Jesus Christ who has laid such tremendous emphasis on hearing. For Him there is nothing mechanical in hearing. It is the response of what a man has made himself. It is the swift reaction of the character, and character is destiny.

In closing I point to another familiar fact which helps to illustrate our text. It is the fact that in the company of certain people there are things that we should never dream of saying. There are people in whose presence the most indecent tongue never feels one vestige of restraint. There are other people in whose hearing one would not venture on an unseemly word. And all that, to the observant mind, indicates that the kind of thing we hear depends in no small measure on the character. If one were to tell me an objectionable story, I should certainly be very much ashamed. But not of the narrator only should I be ashamed; I should be ashamed also of myself. I should be ashamed that he had such thoughts of me, and of the kind of thing I loved to hear, that he would venture on such garbage to amuse me.

There are thousands of men in a city such as this, whose lips are far from being what they ought to be. Yet moving among them every day are citizens who are never visited by their indecency. If their life and character were different, it would all be poured into their ear; but being what they are, they never hear it. To a large extent in our daily life we *are* responsible for what we hear. There are numerous occasions every day when a man is largely to blame for what is told him. He has invited it by his own habits, by all the impress he has made on others. Had he been living a more worthy life his character would have commanded silence. My brother and sister, take heed what you hear. It is often a revelation of yourself. Count it a thing much to be desired that men should honor you with worthy speech. And when they do the opposite, look inward and find what must be amiss in you, when men whose words are dishonoring to God venture to trade upon a fellow-feeling. There is no refuge in silence for a Christian. Silence may only indicate consent. There is no refuge from the strife of tongues save in the fellowship of Jesus Christ. For in His presence all that is evil dies, and gossip and indecency are silent, and something stirs men to say out their worthiest as conscious of a heart that understands.

"Be still, and know that I am God"
(Ps. 46:10).

18
The Ministry of Silence

There are certain voices which we never hear save when everything is silent. They reach us as a revelation of the stillness. Sometimes on a summer afternoon one gets away from city or from village and climbs up the grassy hillside until all the noise of human life is lost, and it is often then that there breaks upon the ear a certain indistinguishable murmur as of the moving of innumerable wings. Travelers tell us that there are rivers flowing beneath the streets of the ancient city of Shechem. During the hours of the day you cannot hear them, for the noise of the narrow streets and the bazaars. But evening comes, the clamor dies away, and the dews of kindly sleep rest on the city. Then quite audibly in the hush of night you may hear the music of the buried streams. There are many voices like those hidden waters. You never can hear them save when things are still. There are whisperings of conscience in the bosom which a very little stir can easily drown. There are tidings from the eternal Spirit who is not far away from any one of us, tidings that will come and go unnoticed, unless we have won the grace of being still.

And yet that very element of stillness is one which is conspicuously lacking now. We have been taught the art of being strenuous, and we have lost the art of being still. A recent writer, in a brilliant essay on the orchestral music of today, tells us that we are living nowadays under "the dominion of din." And whether or not that be true of orchestral music, of which I am not qualified to speak, it is certainly true of ordinary life. Our forefathers in the religious life may have had very imperfect ideals of Christian service. They may have tolerated social abuses which we should never tolerate today. But they had one element in their religious life in an ampler measure than we have it, and that was the blessed element of silence. What peace there was in the old-fashioned Sabbath—what a reverent stillness in the house of God—what a quiet and leisurely solemnity in the morning worship at the family altar! And if today we cannot but be conscious that something of that old spirit has departed, we know that something precious has been lost. It is a gain to be immersed in service. It is a high ambition to be strenuous. "Whatsoever thy hand findeth to do, do it with all thy might" (Eccl. 9:10). And yet the Bible never says to us, "Be strenuous, and know that I am God." It says, "Be still, and know that I am God."

Indeed, so in love are we with noise today that stillness is commonly looked upon as weakness. And it is well to remind ourselves occasionally that often the very opposite is true. When the rain beats against the window pane we are awakened by the driving of it. But the snow falls so silently that never an infant stirs within its cradle. And yet the snow may block up every road quite as effectually as soldiery and dislocate the traffic of a kingdom. Set a thousand scratching spades to work, and you produce a certain effect upon the soil. But now the frost comes with her silent fingers and lightly touches field and meadow with them; and in a single night that silent frost will work more effectually than a thousand spades. God does not work in this strange world by hustling. God works in the world far oftener by hush. In all the mightiest powers which encircle us there is a certain element of stillness. And if I did not find in Jesus Christ something of that divine inaudibility, I confess I should be tempted to distrust Him.

When Epictetus[1] had had his arm broken by the savage cruelty of his master, he turned round without one trace of anger and said to him quietly, *I told you so.* And when a heathen satirist taunted the

---

1. Epictetus (c. A.D. 60–120), Stoic philosopher.

Christians, asking what nobler thing their Master did, one of them answered, *He kept silence*. There is a silence that may speak of weakness. There is another silence that is full of power. It is the empty husk that rattles in the breeze. It is the brook and not the river that goes brawling. And it is well we should remember *that* when we are tempted to associate quietness with weakness, as perhaps we are all tempted nowadays.

There is, of course, a certain kind of silence which is but the outward sign of self-absorption. It does not indicate that a man is hearing anything; it just means that he is withdrawn into himself. I have heard runners say that in great races they have been oblivious of every sound. There may have been a thousand voices cheering them, and yet they seemed to run in a great silence. Perhaps all of us have had hours such as that—hours of suffering or of intense activity—when we felt ourselves alone in a great solitude. That is the stillness of absorption. It is not the stillness to which our text refers. It is of another quietness that it speaks: the quietness which is the basis of communion. For there are times when we never speak so tellingly, and times when we never hear so finely, as when the tongue is silent, the lips are closed, and the spirit is the one interpreter. A love that has no silence has no depth. "Methinks the lady doth protest too much."[2] There are people whose love we instinctively distrust because they are always telling us about it. And perhaps it is simply because God is love, in all the glorious fullness of that word, that we have to be still if we would know Him.

Indeed, there is often no surer sign than silence that the heart has been reached and the depths been broken up. In their greatest hours men are seldom noisy. I have watched sometimes an audience at a concert—for to me the audience is more interesting than the music—I have watched the listless attention which they gave to music that reached no farther than the ear. And then perhaps there was some perfect melody—some chord which had the insistence of a message—and it was as if a voice had cried aloud, *Be still, and know that I am God*. Charles Reade[3] in one of the best of his novels tells a story of some Australian miners. He tells how they traveled through a long summer Sunday to hear the singing of a captive

---

2. From *Hamlet*, Act II; sc. 2, by Shakespeare.
3. Charles Reade (1814–84), English novelist.

thrush. And they were reckless men, familiar with all riot, but when they heard it there fell a hush upon them, for it brought back memories of the green lanes again and of England where they had been boys. In grander fashion that is true of God. We reach Him by the feelings of the heart. We do not clamber to Him by the steps of logic; we reach Him by the feelings of the heart. And it is just because, when the heart is moved profoundly, there falls upon it a silence and a stillness, that we are bidden in our text to be still and know that He is God.

Probably that is the reason, too, why great silences have a divine suggestion. Great silent spaces speak to us of God. I remember a year or two ago visiting the cathedral at Cologne. I suppose it is the most magnificent example of Gothic architecture in the world. And I recall vividly, as though it had happened yesterday, how, passing in from the crowded city streets, the thought of the presence of God was overwhelming. I knew He was present in the teeming city. I knew He was present in the crowded thoroughfare. I knew that where the stir and traffic were, the infinite Spirit was not far away. And yet it is one thing to know, and it is quite another thing to feel; in the calm and solemn quiet of the cathedral I felt that God was there.

That is what spiritual men have always felt under the silence of the starry sky. That is why they have always thought of God when they lifted up their eyes unto the hills. Our noisy talkative life is like the surge breaking on the margin of the shore, and away beyond it is the silent ocean carrying the message of infinity.

We lose our sense of God in a great city far more readily than lonely dwellers do. And we lay the blame of that upon a score of things—on the strain of business, on our abundant pleasures. Perhaps there is a deeper reason than all these; it is the loss of the ministry of silence of the moor and of the glen and of the hill, of the solitudes which are quivering with God. Spare your compassion for the Highland crofter [4]. The man may be far richer than you think. It may be he has kept what we have lost in the keen and eager zest of city life. It may be he has kept in all his poverty those intimations of a present God which are given where a great silence is, as of the lonely moor or of the glen.

---

4. a tenant farmer

The Ministry of Silence

I close by suggesting that this is the reason why God makes silences in every life: the silence of sleep, the silences of sorrow, and then the last great silence at the end. One of the hardest things in the world, as you all know, is to get little children to keep still. They are in a state of perpetual activity, restless, eager, questioning, alert. And just as a mother says to her child, *Be still*, and hushes it to sleep that it may rest, so God does sooner or later with us all. What a quiet, still place the sick-room is! What a silence there is over a house of mourning! How the voices are hushed, and every footstep soft when someone is lying in white within the coffin. Had we the choosing of our own affairs we should never have chosen such an hour as that, and yet how often it is rich in blessing. All the activities of eager years may not have taught us quite so much as that. There are things which we never learn when we are active. There are things which we only learn when we are passive. And so God comes in His resistless way, which never ceases to be a way of love, and says, *Be still, and know that I am God*. If that be so with the passive hours of life, may it not be so with the passive hour of death? What is death but the Almighty Father saying to our talking lips, *Be still*? And I for one believe that in that stillness we shall awaken to know that He is God, in such a love and power as will be heaven.

"If I ascend up into heaven, thou art there: if I make my bed in hell, behold, thou art there" (Ps. 139:8).

19
The Comfort of the Universal Presence

In the library of our University are certain old and interesting maps. They have all the charms of a geography which knows no limit save imagination. In modern atlases, where there is ignorance, such ignorance is handsomely acknowledged. In older atlases, on the contrary, it is curiously and cunningly concealed. And so we read upon these dusty parchments over territories unexplored the fascinating news that here be anthropophagi or satyrs and sundry other goblins. All that has vanished from our ken[1] today, but there is one thing which is left us still: it is that across the map, to the remotest boundary, we can write with full assurance, *Here is God.* If I ascend to heaven, thou art there: if I make my bed in hell, thou art there; if I follow the beckoning of rosy-fingered morn, I am still in the keeping of the eternal Father. Do you and I dwell as we should on that? Do we know the comfort of God's omnipresence? I want to handle that a little, when so many dear to us are far away.

First, then, I ask you to consider that the universal presence is an

---

1. knowledge or perception

arresting thought. There is nothing on earth, when we are tempted sorely, so quietly arresting as a presence. There are times of temptation when the wisest counsel is swept from us like leaves before the gale, times when everything we have resolved upon is broken like a thread of gossamer. And how often, in such times as these, when the wisest counsel has been powerless, we have found restraining power in a presence. It may be the presence of actual proximity. It may be only the presence of the heart, the presence of someone who, for many a year, has been sleeping under the grass of the churchyard. But love is mighty in resurrection-power, and eyes which once we loved are on us still; only God in heaven could tell aright how men have been helped by them when they were tempted.

You remember the story which I have often told you of Frederick Robertson of Brighton;[2] how in Brighton there was a certain shopkeeper who had a portrait of Robertson in his back room. And whenever he was tempted to a mean thing he went and looked for an instant at the photograph, and then the sorry thing became impossible. It was not Robertson's sermons which did that, searching and beautiful although they were. It was not the memory of those flaming words which scorched and shriveled what was bestial. What gripped that man and stayed his itching hand when he was tempted to be less than his true self was the constraining power of a presence. That is often the power of little children. It is often the power of a good woman. We never feel that someone is rebuking; what we feel is that somebody is watching. Eyes are upon us, innocent and tender, eyes that we have not seen for many a year; God knows—*that thing*—we cannot do it.

Now as it is with the presence of our loved ones, so is it with the presence of our God. There is a mighty power to arrest us in the controlling thought that He is here. There is an old story of a little girl who went to the loft to steal the apples there. And on the wall there hung the portrait of some venerable and long forgotten ancestor. And whenever she crept along the garret floor the eyes of that old portrait followed her, until in her childish fear she tore them out. If one could only tear out eyes like that, sin would be infinitely

---

2. Frederick W. Robertson (1816–1863), English lawyer and Anglican minister who died after only six years of influential ministry in Brighton.

sweet for multitudes. But there are eyes no human hand can reach: eyes of memory and eyes of God. And that, I take it, is what Scripture means in that text so often misinterpreted, "I will guide thee with mine eye" (Ps. 32:8). Linnæus,[3] the greatest botanist who ever lived, cherished an open heart for God in everything. Over his study door these words were written: *Numen adest, vivite innocui*. And what they mean is this: Live innocently; do not sully hand nor heart today: *numen adest*—deity is present. Now let me ask you, have you tried to live "as ever in the great Taskmaster's eye"?[4] Have you ever halted in the jostling street and said to yourself, "God is now here"? Say it the next time you are worried, Martha. Say it when the waves are stormy, Peter. Say it, David, when on the roof at evening you catch that glimpse of beautiful Bathsheba. Men who have tempers often excuse themselves; they cannot help it— they are built that way. But if you were in audience with the King, you could control that nasty temper perfectly. And the simple fact is that wherever you are, among the clerks or with your wife and children, you are always in the presence of the King. There is an arresting power in God's presence which few of us have ever really used. It is a great moment when we say with Hagar, "Thou God seest me" (Gen. 16:13). You who this night are very sorely tempted and know it is an hour of crisis for you, One who is infinite love and power and purity is there where you are and is watching.

Passing on a little, I remark, in the second place, that the universal presence is a *sustaining* thought. Professor Henry Drummond[5] used to tell us about a student in the examination-hall. It was an examination of a decisive nature which would largely determine the young fellow's career. And every now and again out of his pocket he took something, gave a glance at it, and then as quietly slipped it back again. The examiner had his suspicions aroused. He stole up quietly for observation. And he saw—what think you—scribbled notes? No, what he saw was not scribbled notes. It was a portrait of someone very dear, who would be dearer still in coming days when, for better or for worse through life's long battle, the two had become one

---

3. Carolus Linnarus (1707–78), Swedish botanist.

4. From "On His Having Arrived at the Age of Twenty-three" by John Milton (1631).

5. Henry Drummond (1851–1897), Scottish clergyman and writer.

The Comfort of the Universal Presence

before the altar. It was not enough that he should have God-speed. He felt he needed something more than that. He felt he needed just what we all need, the sustaining power of a loving presence. And the one presence we can always have, through life and suffering and work and death, is that of the One who loves us to the uttermost. He is with us always, and He is with us everywhere; He is with us when we wake and when we sleep: love infinite, and understanding perfect, and power irresistible that makes the devils tremble. And yet we fret and worry and are fearful and dread tomorrow and vex ourselves in vain, as if all had not been pledged to us in Christ.

I want to say in passing that it is very wonderful what a little thing can make that presence real. It is our proof that God is not a stranger. When a man is a stranger to you and you have never seen him, it is difficult to represent him to yourself. You read his life and go to see his homes, yet after all he is but dim and shadowy. But when you have known a person and when you have loved a person, how different it is from that! A little trifle, and he is here again. Some scrap of writing found in an old pocket—some note of music through an open window, some turn of voice—some quite instinctive gesture—some fragrance as of a flower in summer twilight—these have no power to make present to us one whom we have never known or loved. With one whom we have loved, they are enough.

Now think of that anecdote of Mungo Park,[6] starving and heartless in the sands of Africa. Think how that little tuft of the green moss cried out to his despair that God was there. Such insignificant trifles as the moss could never do that for Park or you or me, unless we came from God who was our home. Probably we loved Him long before we knew. Probably we loved Him in eternity. Trailing clouds of glory do we come from God who is our home. And so, as we take our journey through the world, a thousand trifles that to the beasts are nothing, to us are strange mysterious remembrancers of one whom we have loved long since and lost awhile. There is not a bush but is crying, God is here, not a blossoming tree on any hill. There is not a bird but is singing the same message, not a ripple breaking on the shore. The eyes of children—the love of noble women—the heroism of men who fight and die, speak to us of God

---

6. Mungo Park (1771–1806), Scottish surgeon and explorer noted for his expeditions to Africa.

because we know Him and have the touch of His hand upon our hearts.

I close by observing, in the third place, that in the universal presence is a *uniting* power. Do you ask how a presence can unite? Well, that is not very difficult to answer. Here are a father and mother who have grown estranged. Does the presence of a child never unite them? Did you never hear of them becoming one again through that little living thing? Or here is a young fellow fighting for his country, and now he is wounded and in hospital. And why does he ask his comrade, going home, to be sure to call on his father and his mother? It is because he feels, though he has never reasoned it, that when those who love are separate from each other, there is a wonderful uniting power in a presence. It is so with the presence of a common friend. It is so with the presence of a common God. Separated by a thousand leagues from one another, we are all one in Him. God who is there and here, and yet is one—God who is everywhere and yet our Father—is the only real meeting-ground for mortals, when "seas between us braid hae roared."

When Crimean Simpson,[7] as he is always called, was present at the battle of Sebastopol, suddenly, amid the terrific din, his eye caught a tiny leafy plant, a speedwell at his feet. And in a twinkling his heart was back in Scotland, and he was wandering with Hugh Macdonald there, gathering the blue speedwells on Gleniffer. God is the mystical speedwell of the separated. His is the living presence that unites. In Him we are never distant from each other, although there lie a thousand miles between us. And therefore the need, in such a time as this, when almost every home is rent in twain, that we should live in the presence of the Father.

---

7. Sir George Simpson (1791?–1860), traveler who made a famous "overland" trip around the world in 1841–42.

"Jesus wept" (John 11:35).
"He beheld the city, and wept over it" (Luke 19:41).

20
The Tears of Jesus

There are but two occasions in the Gospels on which we come upon our Savior weeping, only two instances in which we see His tears. It is true that in the Epistle to the Hebrews we have a glimpse into the inner life of Christ, and there we read that He made supplication with tears and strong crying unto God. But into that interior life of prayer, when Father and Son had fellowship together, we cannot enter for it is holy ground. The point to observe is that in His recorded life we only hear of the tears of Jesus twice: once at the grave of a man who was His friend, once when Jerusalem spread out before Him. And both, not in the earlier days of youth when the human heart is susceptible and quivering, but in the later season when the cross was near.

In his autobiography Goethe[1] confesses that as he grew older he lost the power of tears, and there are many men who, as experience gathers, are conscious of a hardening like that. But our Savior, to the last moment that He lived, was quick and quivering to joy and

---

1. Johann Wolfgang von Goethe (1749–1832), German poet, playwright, and philosopher.

sorrow, and His recorded tears are near the end. Never was He so conscious of His joy as in the closing season of His ministry; never did He speak so much about it, nor so single it out as His most precious legacy. And so with weeping, which in the human heart is so often the other side of joy—it is under the shadow of the close it is recorded.

Now I am going to speak for a moment or two on the differences between these two weepings; first I ask you to observe one feature in which the two are beautifully kin. There are tears in the world, bitter and scalding tears, which are wrung out by personal affliction, tears of anguish, of intense corporeal anguish, tears caused by cruelty or mockery. And the point to be ever observed is that our Lord, though He suffered intensely in all such ways as that, never, so far as we read, was moved to tears. He was laughed to scorn—He of the sensitive heart—yet it is not then we read that Jesus wept. He was spat upon and scourged and crucified, but it is not then we light upon Him weeping. And even in the garden of Gethsemane, where great drops were falling to the ground, drops which would have looked like tears to any prying child among the olives, Scripture tells us, as with a note of warning lest we should misinterpret what was happening there, that they were not tears but drops of sweat and blood. The tears of our Lord were not wrung out by suffering, however intense and cruel it might be. On the only two occasions when we read of them, they are the tears of a divine compassion. And whenever one thinks of that, one is impressed again with the wonder of the figure of the Christ, so infinitely pitiful and tender-hearted, so unswervingly and magnificently brave.

Now if we take these two occasions on which the weeping of Jesus is recorded, and if, having found their common element, we go on to note the points on which they differ, what is the difference that first would arrest you? Well, I shall tell you what first impresses me. It is that the former tears were shed for *one*, and the latter tears were shed for *many*. Jesus wept beside the grave of Lazarus for one single solitary friend, for a man who had loved Him with a great devotion and given Him always a welcome in his home. There is no such human touch in all the Gospels, nothing that so betrays the heart of Christ, as to be simply told that Jesus wept when He went out to stand before the grave of Lazarus. Here is a heart that has known the power of friendship, that has known the infinite solace of the *one*—a heart more deeply moved when that one dies than by all the cruelties which men can hurl at Him. And then, having learned His infinite compassion for those who have had one heart to love and lose, we read that Jesus wept *over the city.*

Picture Jerusalem on that Sunday morning, densely crowded for the Passover. Every house was full and every street was thronged; there were tens of thousands gathered there. And it was when our Lord, turning the crest of Olivet, saw before Him that so crowded city, that like summer tempest came His tears. Tears for the one, tears for the twice ten thousand—how typical is that of the Redeemer! Never was there a compassion so discriminative and never a compassion so inclusive. Our separate sorrows—He understands them all and our hours of solitary anguish by the grave, but not less the problem of the crowd. There are men who are full of sympathy for personal sorrows but have never heard the crying of the multitude. There are men who hear the crying of the multitude but have never been brokenhearted at the tomb. Christ has room for all and room for each. He loves the world with a divine compassion. And yet there is no one here who cannot say, "He loved *me*, and gave himself for *me*" (Gal. 2:20).

The next difference which impresses me is this—and it is a suggestive and profound distinction—it is that the former tears were shed for *death*, and the latter tears were shed for *life*. There was something in the death of Lazarus which made a profound impression upon Christ. He was troubled; He groaned in spirit; He wept. Often He had been face to face with death before, with death in some of its most tragic aspects. He had looked on the still cold face of Jairus' daughter and had seen the anguish of the widow of Nain. Yet it is only now, upon the road at Bethany, that we see the storm and passion of His soul when faced by the awful ravages of death. Nobody ever fathoms all that death means until its hand has knocked upon his door. It is when someone whom we have loved is taken that we understand its meaning and its misery.

And now for the first time in all His ministry our Lord had lost *a friend*, and it made death gigantic and appalling. He felt the anguish of it in His soul with an intensity hitherto unknown. Death had come home to Him—attacked Him at close quarters—carried one of the bastions of His being. And in that hour our Savior realized, as He had never realized before, how utterly cruel was the last great enemy. It was then He groaned in spirit and was troubled; a storm of passion swept across His soul. It was then He wept for all that death had done, and all that death was doing in the world. And so these tears of His are sacramental of all the sorrow of the aching heart when the place is empty, the grave is tenanted, and the familiar voice is silent.

Now with that dark and dreary scene will you for a moment contrast the other scene? It is a city shimmering in beauty under the radiance of a Sunday morning. Children are playing in the marketplace; women are singing as they rock the cradle; men are at business and regiments are marching—there is movement, and there is music everywhere. Friends are meeting who have not met for years for Passover was the great season of reunion. Eyes are bright, and hearts are beating bravely in the gladness of these old ties reknit. Out on the Bethany road there had been *death*; here in the teeming city there was *life*: life in the crowd, life in the marching soldiery, life in the little children romping merrily, and life everywhere in the indistinguishable murmur which rises where there are ten thousand people who have waked in the sunshine of another morning to the traffic and the concourse of the day. It was all that which swept into the gaze of Christ, and it was that which swept into the heart of Christ that Sunday morning when from the brow of Olivet He looked across the valley to Jerusalem.

As a lad of twelve He had looked and looking wondered, with all the thrilling expectancy of boyhood. Now we read that He looked and looking, wept. They were not tears for death but tears for life: tears of divine compassion for the living; tears for the might have been—the vanity—the awful judgment that was yet to be; tears for the living who have gone astray, who are hungering for peace and have missed it, and who have had their opportunity and failed. My friend, there is a sorrow for the dead which may be intense and very tragic. It may wither every flower across the meadow and take all the summer sunshine from the sky.

But there is a sorrow deeper than sorrow for the dead—it is the sorrow for the living; it is much to know that Jesus understood it. The bitterest sorrow has no grave to stand at, no sepulcher to adorn with opening flowers; the bitterest sorrow wears no garb of mourning and springs from that mystery which we call life, and Jesus felt it to His depths. You who are mourning for the dead tonight, for you there is

Jesus by the grave of Lazarus. You who are mourning for the living, for you also is that same compassion. He understands it all. He shares it. Like a great tide it flowed upon Him once, when in the morning from the brow of Olivet, He looked upon Jerusalem and wept.

I close by pointing out one other difference that stands out very clearly in the Scripture. The former tears were such *as others shared in*; the latter were tears *that no one understood.* Read that chapter in the Gospel of John again, and you find that Christ was not alone in weeping. Martha and Mary were there, and they were weeping also along with the Jews who had known Lazarus and loved him. There was a kinship in a common sorrow there, a fellow-feeling which united hearts, a sense of common loss and ache and loneliness.

Now turn to the other scene, and what a difference! It is a pageantry of enthusiastic gladness. The cry goes ringing along the country road, "Hosanna to the Son of David." And it is amid these shouting voices of men beside themselves with wild enthusiasm that the Scripture tells us Jesus wept. At the grave of Lazarus many an eye was wet. Here every eye was dancing with excitement. No one was weeping here, nobody thought of weeping; it was the triumph of the Lord—Hosanna! And all alone amid that welcoming tumult in a grief which nobody could pierce or penetrate, the tears came welling from our Savior's eyes.

In this our mortal life there are common griefs, touches of nature which make the whole world kin. But how endlessly true is the old saying of Scripture that the heart knows its own bitterness. And in those bitternesses which words can never utter and which lie too deep for any human help, what a comfort to know that our Savior understands! In all the common sorrows of humanity He is our brother, and He weeps with us. He stands beside the grave of Lazarus still, clothed in the beauty of His resurrection. But in that lonely unutterable sorrow which is the price and the penalty of personality, we may be sure He understands us also.

"We returned all of us to the wall, every one unto his work" (Neh. 4:15).

21
On Taking Things Up Again

That seems a very simple thing to do, and yet it had the seeds of heroism in it. It was one of those quiet and unillumined actions which are greater than they seem. It was an arduous and stupendous business, that business of building again these ruined walls. Even if all the conditions had been favorable, it would have been a Herculean task. But the difficulties were enormously augmented by the fact that there were enemies on every hand, watching the builders with intense malevolence. The kind of atmosphere that we are working in makes a vast difference to our work. Tasks that would be comparatively light if there were sympathy become insupportable among suspicions. And that is how we can all help each other in bearing the burdens of the common day—by showing that we understand and can appreciate.

To do one's duty quietly and serenely when tongues are scurrilous and eyes suspicious, never to lose one's purpose or one's peace though everything that one does is misinterpreted—it may be that in the eye of heaven there is as great a fortitude in that as in any gallant action of the battlefield. Now that is what strikes one about Nehemiah. He had very preeminently that kind of courage. He was not in any respect a brilliant man; but he was undoubtedly a dogged man. And nowhere in this interesting little book do we see that doggedness of his more useful than in the incident recorded in our text.

It happened, too, just at that very time when discouragements are apt to multiply. It happened, as an earlier verse informs us, when the building of the walls was half completed. With all the enthusiasm of newborn fervor they had laid the foundation a certain time before. And after a season when the last course was laid, there came all the rejoicings of the cope-stone. But now, the enthusiasm of the start had died away; the gladness of the end was yet unborn; the work of building was in that middle stage which is often the most trying stage of all.

It is so with every creative work. It is so with warfare, and it is so with life. There is a middle period in everything which is most perilous and most discouraging. It is the time when the hopeful ardor of beginnings has died down into the light of common day, and when the ear has not been quickened yet to the music of the distant triumph-song. Whatever the wall that you are toiling at, expect discouragement about the middle stages. Lay your account for that and be prepared. You cannot have always the glory of the morning. He who comes smiling from the world's snare uncaught is not the man who starts with shrilling trumpets, but he who has learned, as Nehemiah learned, to hold to it in the mid-watch of the day.

> Tasks in hours of insight willed,
> May be through days of gloom fulfilled.

That is the only way, given among men, to bring our days of gloom into the sunshine. To trample underfoot all moods and feelings, to get to our appointed work in spite of them is the one way to power and freedom here and at last to the sunrise and the crown.

But our text does not only speak of dogged labor; it speaks also of a return to labor. Let me explain to you the contextual setting of our words. There came a time when the wall was about half built and when the enemies of Nehemiah ceased to jeer. There came a time when they banded themselves together to hinder action by the force of arms. And Nehemiah, when he learned of this, and with all the swiftness of a born commander, stopped everything; he summoned every workman, set them in companies, and armed them for resistance. As often happens, readiness meant safety. The advancing enemy withdrew. Faced by military where they looked for masons, discretion became the better part of valor. And it was then, as Nehemiah tells us in that quiet way which all true generals have, that "we returned to the wall, every man to his work."

Now I want you to try to picture to yourselves all that lies hidden behind that quiet statement—the excitement, and the call to arms, and the unsettlement of military training. I want you to try to picture the unrest that would seize upon every heart in such an hour that you may understand the heroism of our text. There are few things so unsettling in this life as a mighty outburst of military ardor. Under its throbbing, our common daily drudgeries seem in an hour a thousand miles away. Yet here, the moment the alarm was over and the tidings brought of a retreating enemy, "we returned to the wall, every man to his work." It betrays a spirit which is not lightly moved. It betrays the spirit we all need. He who can so return to quiet drudgery is on the highway to be morally victorious. It is not enough if a man would win his soul that he should learn to do battle with his sins. He must also learn to master those unsettlements from which nobody is exempted.

I think, for instance, that we all need that spirit when we come back to town again after our vacations. A vacation is a very blessed business; but it may also be a most unsettling business. As the years pass, and we grow older, such unsettlement is less accentuated. It is one of the compensations that we gain for the loss of the earlier intensities of feeling. Yet even to the end it is not easy, after a time of sunshine and of liberty, to come back to the dreary round again in the school or the office or the shop. A little knowledge is a dangerous thing, and a little liberty may be a dangerous thing— those sunny mornings when every hour is free through the long reaches of an unfettered day. And then, when it is only just beginning, and the touch of it is making music in the heart—the building of that dreary wall again. I have known men who would never take a vacation, they were so afraid of that unsettlement. And I have known men who after a summer's liberty did not get into their stride again for weeks. But the victorious spirit for all such hours of life is just that quiet and uncomplaining fortitude which will take every crowded hour of life God gives and then come quietly to the wall again. Those workmen of Nehemiah were twice active when they returned from their brief essay of arms. There was something of the warrior in each of them; you could have seen it in the han-

On Taking Things Up Again

dling of their tools. And so we all, enriched by summer memories of moor and sea and sky, of love and laughter, are to be twice the servants we ever were before.

I think, too, we all need that spirit after a time of sorrow. There is a strange unsettlement about all hours of sorrow which makes the common working very irksome. Across in beautiful France these autumn days, the great guns have made terrific havoc. The familiar poplars along the roads are torn; there are horrible pits and gashes in the fields.[1] And then the peasant comes creeping back again to the scenes that he has known and loved since infancy—and they are changed; he can hardly recognize them; the familiar landmarks are all vanished. That is the shattering work of great artillery, and that is often the shattering work of sorrow. It changes things, alters every aspect, and draws great gashes across familiar places. And so it is often a very difficult thing, when the heart in sorrow has been smitten sorely, to come to the daily drudgery again.

In such sorrowful and darkened hours we must remember Nehemiah's workmen. We are not here to brood upon our sorrows. We are here to feel that God is in them all. We are here to turn again out of the darkness to the burden-bearing of the common day, as the builders of Nehemiah to their toil. When the daughter of Jairus was raised to life again, Christ commanded that something be given her to eat (Luke 8:55). I think He did that for the mother's sake, just as much as for the daughter's. What wiser order could He have given the mother, in the wild unsettlement of such an hour, than just to get something ready in the kitchen? It is through such common tasks that we are steadied. Through the routine we see the stars again. We master our sorrows not by brooding on them; we master our sorrows by our duties. And therefore the need for every one of us, amid the shock and change and tragedy of things, of that quiet heroism which returns to the appointed duty of the day.

I think also that in peculiar measure such a spirit is needed in this hour. In a time of national excitement like the present we ought to remember Nehemiah's workmen. For long and fruitful years we lived in peace. We went to our daily labors in security.

---

1. This message was preached during World War I and the terrible battles in Europe.

And summer and winter passed, the birds came north again, and life was even and quiet in its tenor. But now, since the news of war flashed around the world, what a different world it is that we are living in! We are intensely stirred and tossed out of the usual, and we know not what an hour may bring forth. I am not thinking of the young men just now to whom the call has come to serve their country. Of them we are proud; they have been true to duty, and they will be better and nobler to their dying hour. I am thinking of all of us who are at home and who cannot take up arms and serve like that; all of us who because of circumstances must stay behind. For us there is none of the peril of the field, and for us none of the glory of the field. There will be none to crowd the street and cheer us wildly when the day is over and the flag is furled. Our duty, our first and foremost duty, is to have it said of us as of these builders, that morning by morning, through fair report and foul, we returned to the wall, every man to his work. That is the fortitude which is required of us. Let us see to it that it be not lacking.

In daily and uneventful drudgery let us be twice as faithful as we were before. Through personal sorrows and family anxieties, through tidings of victory or of disaster, here is our duty, and we shall do our duty until the day break and the shadows flee away. My delicate friend, if you act like that, you shall not walk the street as one ashamed. You shall not have an unhappy conscience when your more fortunate comrades come to their homes again. For you too in quiet lowly ways shall have fought your way to fidelity of service, and in the bloodiest field where men are fighting there is no service worthier than that. To take up one's *rifle* may be a hard thing. To take up one's *cross* may be a harder thing: to take it up every morning patiently, in the teeth of all excitement and unsettlement. And that is why in these so stirring days when the music of the trumpet is abroad, I want you quietly, patiently, and bravely to return to the wall, every man to his work.

I close by remarking that this quiet return was preeminently characteristic of our Savior. Studying the footsteps of our blessed Lord, you come upon periods of profoundest stirring. You come upon periods, if I might put it so, when He was thrilled to the finest fiber of His being. You come upon days when the deeps were broken up, when the windows of heaven were opened wide

On Taking Things Up Again

above Him, when a tempest seems to have swept across His soul. Now it was out in the desert all alone; now it was when transfigured on the mountain; now it was when the Greeks came seeking Him; now it was by the grave of Lazarus.

And what one always notices is this, that when the great unsettlement is over, our Lord is back again at His familiar service of loving and beautiful and lowly deeds. It is all told with such exquisite simplicity that we might readily miss the quiet heroism of it. And yet for the seeing eye in all the life of Christ, there is perhaps nothing more wonderful than that—the quiet and unfaltering perseverance in the way of duty and the cross. May we all have grace to follow in His steps. It is the only road that makes for liberty. Through sorrow—joy—unsettlement—excitement, may we return to the wall, every man to his work. And then for us too, though no man ever hear of us and we win no place on any roll of honor, at sunset, when the stars come out, there will be, "Well done, good and faithful servant" (Matt. 25:21).

"Thou shalt not desire the silver or gold that is on them [the idols]" (Deut. 7:25).

22
The Silver on the Idol

The fiercest struggle which Israel had to wage was the struggle to maintain its spirituality. It was in constant peril of declining on the degrading practices of idol-worship. Surrounded by the ancient rites of Egypt there had come a silent sapping of the heart. Influences never to be quite eradicated had seeded in the life of captive Israel. And now, about to enter the new country where was to be their triumph and their tragedy, influences still more deadly were inevitable. Everywhere in the promised land of Canaan the practices of idolatry were rife. Every grove had its polluting worship; every hill its altar or its shrine. And hence the severity, the ring of ruthlessness, the fierce rejection of the thought of compromise that sounds through these injunctions of the Lord.

Now there was one problem certain to emerge in that long struggle of extermination, and it is this problem which in our text the care of heaven foresees and makes provision for. Many of the idols of the Canaanites were fashioned with curious and costly workmanship. There was exquisite work of silver on their surface; there was delicate artistry of beaten gold. And the question was, when the Canaanites were vanquished and their idols had fallen into the victors' hands, how were these precious things to be regarded? Every one knew what had occurred in Egypt. The spoiling of the Egyptians was commanded. With jewels of silver and ornaments of gold Israel had journeyed from the house of bondage. And the problem was, were they to act in Canaan as they had been bidden by God to act in Egypt and to enrich themselves with idol-spoil? It was then that clear and sharp came the command. You shall not desire their silver or their gold. Let them alone. Lay not a hand upon them. Burn them in the fire until they be perished. No Jewish woman was to adorn herself, no house was to be adorned, no temple beautified with the gold or with the silver of the idol.

Nor is it difficult to recognize the wisdom which was embodied in that divine command. It is God's recognition of the tremendous power that is exerted by association. Certain things may in themselves be harmless, and yet for you they may be far from harmless. Certain words may in themselves be innocent, and yet they can never be innocent for you. For old associations cling to them and something that once happened is recalled, and for you they shall always carry some suggestion that is not pure nor beautiful nor worthy. Such was the peril of this gold and silver. Subtly but surely it would suggest the idol. Disguise it how they might, it would recall the dark associations of its origin. Women would wear the gold upon their persons and lovingly handle the ornament of silver, and swift as an arrow-flight their thought would travel to the idol from which it had been torn.

"First," says Thomas á Kempis[1] of temptation—"first there cometh a bare thought of sin." That is how sin begins, whose end is misery—in the sudden flash of a thought, in a suggestion. And so the Maker of the human heart, who knows what gateways into hell it has, cries out in the very agony of tenderness, "Thou shalt not desire their silver or their gold." God has no quarrel with that silver filigree. He is the perfect lover of the beautiful. But there is one thing that He loves still more than beauty, and that is the spiritual welfare of His children. And so in exquisite sympathy He cautions them and summons them to a rigorous abstention, not because of hatred for the silver but because of compassion for His sons. I want, then, to take that principle tonight and to try to show its bearings upon life.

---

1. Thomas á Kempis (1379–1471), German monk and author or copyist of *The Imitation of Christ*.

To begin with, let us think of literature; let us apply that principle to literature. If books like idols are doing the devil's work, we are not to desire their silver or their gold. Now I am not a precisian in regard to reading. I would allow to every man an ample liberty. I see no reason in the world to be a pessimist in regard to the state of literature today. Still the fact remains, and you all know it, that books are issued from the press today as redolent of what is base and bestial as any idol of the Canaanites. There are books that should never have been written, and there are books that never should be read. They soil the fingers by the very touch of them; they do more than that, they soil the minds. They tamper lightly with those eternal verities which alone keep life from being dust and ashes. They drag into the light those hidden things which God in His large silences has shrouded. Now if such books were always poor productions, our text would not apply to them at all. No one would read them or ever want to read them. They would be tossed aside contemptuously.

But the very peril of such books is this, that sometimes, like the idols of antiquity, they are adorned with filigree of silver and beautiful with beaten work of gold. How light and delicate the writer's touch—how exquisite the literary style. What clever suggestion of a present heaven amid the passion and excess of hell. And it is when a man who loves all that is beautiful finds himself drawn by these delightful qualities, that his conscience and his God begin to cry to him, *Thou shalt not desire their silver or their gold.* A bad book never should be written, and a bad book never should be read. No charm of style nor literary grace can ever redeem it from its essential villainy. Let it alone. Treat it with contempt. There are things more precious than literary cleverness. There is the strength which is as the strength of ten, because the heart is pure.

The same great principle of circumspection applies, again, to the question of our callings. Every young man should keep it clear before him when he is thinking of what his calling is to be. In the expansion of our modern life the range of possible callings is amazing. Every new discovery or invention means the opening of new careers. One wonders sometimes what people found to do, and where the bread and shoes for children came from in the great cities a hundred years ago. Now in all that multiplicity of labor it is very difficult to make distinctions. It is never easy in its exceeding intricacy to say that *this* is right and *that* is wrong. But none the less in every great community there are always callings dubious and questionable which are not easy to be reconciled with a sensitive and an honorable heart. Now if such callings were lean and hungry things our text would not apply to them at all. But you know how often their very charm is this, that they seem by an easy way to promise riches.

And so God comes to us, as to the Israelites tempted by the adorning of idols, and says in a love that seeks our very highest, *Thou shalt not desire their silver or their gold.* It is not that He has any quarrel with the silver. It is that He has a great compassion for His children. He knows the deadening and fatal influence exerted by association. He knows how silently the best will wither, and all the buoyancy of life be lost if conscience be uneasy in the mind. Let it alone, my brother. Do not touch it. It is always perilous to play with conscience. Better a person without a single ornament than one made beautiful by idol gold. For idol gold can never comfort you, nor bring you any cheer when days are dark, nor give you what is so infinitely sweet—the gladness of the sunshine on the grass.

I think, again, this principle is needful when we are tempted to explore what life is. Men fling themselves into life, as they express it, for the sake of the enrichment which it brings. When Eve was tempted in her Orient paradise, it was not the apple that was her real temptation. I do not imagine she was so fond of apples that she would have risked for one her husband and her God. The fierce temptation for her woman's heart lay in the freedom which was behind the fruit, in the enrichment and enlargement of her being which the eating of it was to bring. To her the apple in itself was nothing. To her the enrichment which it brought was everything.

She craved expansion in her restricted paradise, and she would have it although she disobeyed. And we are often tempted, just as Eve was tempted, to break the bounds that God has placed around us in the craving for a larger, fuller life. It is not the idol which we really want; it is the gold and silver on the idol. It is the new experience, the fresh sensation, the life that is fuller than our dreary round. And so are we tempted from the line of duty on to those dubious or forbidden paths whose end is always emptiness and tears. My brother and sister, you may be sure of this, that it is never thus that God enriches life. Your way is given you, and to rebel against it is never the avenue to liberty. Take up your cross and do not envy others. What is that to you?—follow Me. You shall not desire their silver or their gold.

And then in closing, we should apply our text to the all-important matter of our friendships. For a friendship may play havoc with our life, or it may bring it to the very gates of heaven. To have a friend is to have hidden treasure. It is as water in a weary land. But to have a friend whose character proves worthless is one of the bitterest of life's revealings. And yet how often a very worthless character, just like the graven idols of the Canaanites, is beautiful with silver and with gold. Men may be very clever and be vile. Men may be very brilliant and be false. Men may be utterly untrustworthy and yet be the most delightful of companions. And it is when attracted by such charms as these in a character radically false and vicious that the command still rings upon the ear—*Thou shalt not desire their silver or their gold.* "If thy right hand offend thee, cut it off. If thy right eye offend thee, pluck it out" (Matt. 5:29–30). A friend who is morally worthless is a snare though he have gifts as shining as an angel's. It is never by such bonds that life is blessed. It is never by such ties that strength is won. It is never in such comradeships as these that we lift up our eyes unto the hills.

"I am meek and lowly in heart"
(Matt. 11:29).

23
Humility Interpreted by Christ

It has been said that the greatest of all differences between ancient and modern morality is not the introduction of new virtues but the changing of the order of the old ones. In this sphere, as in other spheres, Christ has put down the mighty from their seats. He has taken the little one of ancient ethics and made it as it were a thousand. And so it is said our Christian morality is not generically different from others; the difference is mainly one of emphasis. Now in this there is a large element of truth and of very fruitful and suggestive truth. No one will ever understand the Savior who forgets how largely He wrought by rearranging. But there is one point at which it is not true and that the most important point of all perhaps—it is not true in reference to humility. Humility was not a virtue in the old world. Humility in the old world was a vice. It was a thing abhorred and accursed, utterly unworthy of the gentleman. And the amazing thing is that in Christendom it has not merely ceased to be a vice but has been given the primacy of virtue. To be humble was once to be contemptible; now to be humble is to be blessed. It was once rejected as a thing of shame; it is now sought for as a grace of heaven. In every communion of universal Christendom, however deep the cleavages between them, the queen of Christian graces is humility.

Now for this Christian glorying in humility there are two reasons which suggest themselves. The first is the expansion given to life by the revelation of our faith. Had you lived within a little room and then been brought under the open heaven, can you not picture how your thought would change in that amazing moment of expansion? Seeing the sun and moon in all their beauty, the azure heaven, and the myriad stars, you would be silent and wonder and adore. Feelings hitherto repressed would awaken; thoughts would rise and soar into the infinite. In a world so high and wonderful and great there would be known the surge of aspiration. And that is exactly what our faith has done in giving *life* its infinite horizon: chords which were silent have begun to vibrate.

Life is not less mysterious since Christ came; it is far more mysterious since Christ came. He has made it high as heaven and deep as hell and touched it to the issues of eternity. And so has been born our Christian aspiration which neither Greek nor Roman ever knew, and humility is the other side of aspiration. Make life a finite and measurable thing, and inevitably you foster self-complacency. Make it an infinite and eternal thing, and humility ceases to be a thing of scorn. It is the fitting attitude of mind and spirit for one who stands in the light of immortality, and whose true horizon is the eternal God.

And yet that reason, though a very real one, is after all but a secondary one. The primary reason is not our new horizon: it is the personality of Christ. When you meet a person for the first or second time, you may receive from him varying impressions. But gradually, as acquaintance ripens, one clear and definite impression comes. And so as men meditated on the Lord and came to know Him through such meditation, one feature took precedence over all. It was not His courage, although He was very brave; it was not the eloquence with which He spoke. It was not even that mighty power of God with which He healed the sick and raised the dead. Clear and conspicuous above all other qualities, the crown and inspiration of them all, stood out the perfect humility of Jesus. Men found it in every action which He wrought; they lit on it in every word He uttered. They traced it in a thousand subtle touches that are more delicate than speech and action.

It was that large and overwhelming impress, forever deepening as they brooded on it, which altered the conception of mankind. All the humility of Christendom really runs back to that of Christ. If it is the distinguishing virtue of the saint, it was first the distinguishing virtue of the Savior. And that is why to understand humility we must study it in the person of our Lord. Let me use first the method of exclusion.

To begin with, then, the humility of Jesus was certainly not a mean and groveling spirit. The bitterest enemy of the Redeemer has never taunted Him with that. In one of his so pathetic letters the poet Keats says, "I hate humility." You have only to read the context of that letter to discover what he meant by that. He meant that groveling and cringing spirit which Heine[1] called the virtue of a hound and which is immortalized in English literature in the portrait of Uriah Heep.[2] That is what Aristotle would have called humility. That is what Cicero would have called humility. And there are multitudes still who have a lurking feeling that if not the truth, it is very near the truth.

I want you to learn how utterly astray are all such conceptions of humility if the standard of humility be Christ. Christ never groveled before man or God. He never cringed to any living creature. There was a dignity about His bearing which never forsook Him in His darkest hour. It made itself felt among the hardened soldiery, cast its subduing power upon Pilate, touched the Roman centurion to reverence, and awed the clamorous rabble in Gethsemane. I therefore learn that true humility has nothing to do with cringing or with fawning. The moment you associate it with that, you dissociate it from the person of the Lord. For He was a king, had a royal bearing, and moved among His fellows with authority. All the time His humility was perfect.

Going a little further, we must note that the humility of Christ was not self-depreciation. It was not the habit of belittling Himself or the work which God had given Him to do. There were some things which Christ made very light of—things He refused to reckon as important. But there was one thing which He never once made light of and that was the work which was given Him to do. On the contrary, He always magnified it and used the loftiest terms in speaking of it, associating it forever with His glory. Other teachers call men to their message; Jesus called men to Himself. The self-assertion of our

---

1. Heinrich Heine (1792–1856), German poet, critic and journalist.
2. The villanous clerk in Dicken's *David Copperfield*.

Savior is the most magnificent self-assertion in all history. And yet He tells us in this single glimpse which He gives us into the secret of His being, that He is meek and lowly in heart. Clearly, then, the humility of Christ was not any belittling of Himself. It was as far removed from pride on the one hand as from self-depreciation on the other. And it is needful to remember this, for we are often tempted to think that we are humble when all the time we are but doing dishonor to the faculties or the work which God has given us.

Going deeper still, there is one other thing which I beg you very carefully to note. It is that the humility of Christ did not arise from any sense of sin. In your experience and in mine, my friends, there is nothing so humbling as the power of sin. You have had seasons, and I have had seasons when sin has humbled us into the very dust. And that experience, oftentimes repeated and in a measure always present with us, has led us to connect the two together.

Now most unquestionably there is that connection, and most unquestionably God meant it so. It is a blessed hour of true humility when we cry, "God be merciful to me a sinner" (Luke 18:13). But to understand the meaning of humility in all the depth and compass of its glory, we must never forget that it was first exhibited in one who had no sense of sin at all.

The one thing that you cannot find in Christ is any trace of a scar upon His conscience. There was not one single shadow of remorse. There was not one single whisper of regret. Many a cry of prayer was on His lips and went ringing heavenward among the hills, yet the one prayer He never prayed was, "God be merciful to me a sinner." The point to note is that our Lord was sinless and yet was the perfect exemplar of humility. Utterly untouched by moral evil, He was humbler than man has ever been. And that should teach us that this queenly grace is something nobler than the fruit of guilt, however the consciousness of guilt may deepen it.

What, then, was the humility of Christ? Has He Himself thrown any light upon the matter? There are two incidents which at once suggest themselves as teaching us everything we want to know.

On one occasion the disciples had been arguing as to who was greatest in the kingdom. They came to Jesus with their difficulty, and the answer which they received was very beautiful. For Jesus beckoned to a little child, and set him down right in the midst of them, and said, "Whoso humbleth himself as this little child, the same is the greatest in the kingdom of heaven" (Matt. 18:4). There is the living example of humility as Jesus understood humility. And what is the spirit of a little child: is it not a spirit eminently trustful? It trusts a father's wisdom without questioning, confides unfalteringly in a mother's care, and rests in happy security on this, that there is someone arranging and providing. There is nothing mean or groveling in that. In that there is nothing of self-depreciation. A child is not humble because it knows its guilt. It is humble because it is a child. It is humble because it trusts so utterly, because it leans its weight upon a father, because it answers so unswervingly to every movement of another will.

Now that, I take it in its essence, is the humility of Jesus Christ. It is not primarily a relationship to men; primarily it is a relationship to God. It has been noted that in the gospels you do not read about the *faith* of Jesus; what you do read of in the gospels is the *humility* of Jesus. And the reason for that is that our Lord's humility, when you come to understand its inner meaning, is just His faith in its most glorious exercise. Moment by moment He learned the will of God. Moment by moment He responded to it. The faintest whisper of His Father's voice was answered in unquestioning obedience.

And this not only when that will was sweet and reached Him amid the fields of Nazareth, but when it came to Him in the garden of Gethsemane. That was not courage, though it may look like courage. It was not heroism, though you may call it so. It was the perfected spirit of the child whom Jesus took and placed among them all. That was humility as Jesus understood it—loyal, loving, unquestioning submission, not only when submission was a happy thing, but when it led to the garden and the cross.

And you see at once, taking that view, how it explains a great deal which was dark before. It helps us to see the humility of Christ where otherwise we might be blind to it. When a man is humble he is always humble. His humility makes itself evident in everything. You must be able to trace it through his whole activity if it be a real and genuine humility. And yet there are moments in the life of Jesus when it would be difficult to call Him humble in the usual interpretation of that word. Think of His withering anger at the Pharisees. Think of His driving the traders from the Temple. Is *that* humility—that withering anger, or has Christ forgotten to be humble now? No, He has not forgotten to be humble: it is you and I who have forgotten something—forgotten that the humility of Christ is His absolute fidelity to God.

Do you think it was pleasant to Jesus to be angry so? Do you think He delighted to wither and to burn? A thousand times rather, we may say with reverence, He would have been seated in the home at Bethany. Had He consulted self He would have been with Lazarus, among the hills, or in the fields of Galilee; but He withered and burned and drove the traders forth, because He consulted nobody but God. In other words, He was never more a child than in those hours when He seemed least a child. He was never humbler in His Father's eyes than in His awful and imperious majesty. For then you hear, clear as a trumpet note, "I come to do thy will, O God" (Luke 22:42), and that was the humility of Jesus. Take that view, and it irradiates everything. It gives a unity we never felt before. Christ is no longer humble in His suffering, and He is something else in His denunciation. He is as humble when He scorns the Pharisee as when He talks with the woman by the well; as humble when He commands, "Take these things hence," as when He cries upon the cross, "Father, forgive them" (Luke 23:34).

And then there is the second scene which is needed if our thought is to be adequate. It is that scene, forever memorable, in which Jesus washed the disciples' feet. Need I recall it? You all know it perfectly. You see it before you even as I speak: how Jesus laid aside His garments, took a towel and girded Himself and washed His disciples' feet. And He did it "because he was come from God, and because he was going home again to God" (John 7:28, 33) —that is to say, all filial life in God must issue in lowly and loving service. First the *child*, you see, and then the *servant*. Take both together and you have humility. First the child, the filial trustful confidence; and then, as the fruit of that, the servant's office. And that is exactly what you find in Jesus whom the prophet calls the servant of the Lord, and yet says that a little child shall lead them. Perfect loyalty to the Father's will issuing in lowliest service to the family of believers—that was the humility of Christ, and that the humility he wants in us. There is nothing cringing in it, nothing mean. It is trustful, active, eminently blessed. It is the crowning grace of every Christian character and makes the wilderness blossom as the rose.

"In the year that king Uzziah died I saw the Lord . . . and the house was filled with smoke" (Isa. 6:1, 4).

24
The Smoke in the Temple

A few words will make plain to us the circumstances of this vision; it is one of the memorable visions of the world. It happened in the year when King Uzziah died, a year never to be forgotten by the prophet. It is such things that give our truest reckoning; we do not reckon by the first of January. We reckon by the year when sorrow came, or when love came caroling across the heather. The years we date by are not the years of months; they are the years of certain great experiences, when we met somebody when we first did something, when somebody who was everybody died.

In such an hour when his heart was heavy, Isaiah went into the temple. It is the fitting place for every man to go to in the season when the deeps are broken up. There are people who cannot bring themselves to church in the period of an overmastering sorrow. They stay at home, shun the sanctuary, and nurse their lonely misery in solitude. But if there is ever a time in human life not to forsake the assembling of ourselves together, it is just the season when the grave is open. Then is there new meaning in the prayers; then is the music charged with new significance. Then in the commonplaces of the preacher is there something fresh and wonderful and personal. So true is it that we "aye get what we bring," that beauty is in the eye of the beholder, and that we only hear, in this strange world of voices, things which the spirit is attuned to hear. The Lord is in His holy temple, says the psalmist. He was there from the very hour when it was built. He was there when the leaves were green upon the trees and when the land of Judah was in the grip of winter. But even an Isaiah could not see Him in His sovereignty and in His glory until the year that King Uzziah died.

I mention that as a lesson had in passing, but to me there is another lesson here. "In the year that King Uzziah died I saw the Lord," and then immediately *the house was filled with smoke*. In former days there had been no obscurity. Every object had been clearly visible. *There* was the laver, *there* the splendid altar, and *there* the priests plying their daily services. And now for the first time in all his life there fell as it were an obscuring haze on everything, and it fell in the hour in which he saw the Lord. The temple was not brighter than before; somehow the temple was darker than before. The house was not flooded with a radiant glory; the house was filled with smoke. Yesterday he saw the altar perfectly and followed every movement of the priests; today there was an obscurity on everything. The strange thing is that he had this experience in the season when he saw the Lord. It followed hard on the beatific vision. It was the corollary of his ecstasy. He had seen the king—the light of light—the only radiance of earth and heaven; and yet the darkness deepened upon everything.

Now it seems to me as I look out on life, that that is far from being a rare experience. It is like that of the psalmist when he cried, "I remembered God and was troubled" (Ps. 77:3). When Paul on his road to Damascus met with Christ and saw His glory brighter than the sun, did he cry aloud exultingly, "In thy light I see light"? What actually happened was that Paul was blinded and could not see his neighbor or his chariot and had to be led by the hand into the city. Like Isaiah, he too had seen the Lord, exalted and sovereign and glorious. And like Isaiah, having seen the Lord, for him too the house was filled with smoke. Things grew dark that yesterday were plain, and forms and figures were no longer visible. The shadows deepened in the sight of God. Now it is true, and true forever, that to know God is eternal life. Wherever He is known *there,* there is glory. He is the light of the world. And yet how much there is in

The Smoke in the Temple

human life that interprets and explains Isaiah's sequence: "I saw the Lord, *and the house was filled with smoke.*"

One might think, for instance, of that singular change that has been wrought in humanity by Christendom. To pass from ancient Greece into the heart of Christendom is like passing from sunshine into shadow. In ancient Greece the atmosphere was clear. Life was beautiful; it was not mysterious. Man was a finite being, exquisitely formed, happy as a playful child is happy. And then the world awoke and saw the Lord, high and lifted up upon the cross, and immediately the house was filled with smoke. Life has not grown simpler from that hour. Life has grown more mysterious from that hour. It has lost its definite outline of the years and become a thing of infinite significance. It is haunted by voices we but faintly hear, quickened by presences we but dimly see, touched by the awful issues of eternity. Depths have been opened man never dreamed of once. Sin in Christendom has become exceeding sinful. Death is more terrible—suffering more intense—the shadow of guilt is infinitely deepened. And it is when I brood on things like these, that there rings on my ear again this prophet's word: "In the year that King Uzziah died I saw the Lord, *and the house was filled with smoke.*"

One might illustrate that change in many ways: from religious architecture, for example. Is there anybody here tonight who has seen an ancient Greek or Roman temple? If so, you have looked upon a thing of beauty which is a joy forever. Strength is there in those majestic pillars, infinite grace in tracery and finial; everywhere there is exquisite proportion, and the symmetry of part with part is perfect. Yet you and I could never worship there nor feel that God was there nor bow before Him, because in that old temple is no mystery.

Now pass through our crowded city streets and enter our old and beautiful cathedral. It is not perfect. There are disproportions in it. There are curious lapses from a perfect symmetry. Yet how it awes the heart, that noble building, and solemnizes it and speaks of God, in its shadow and its silence and its mystery. There in the frozen melody of stone is the change that has been wrought by seeing God. Awe has come, and aspiration infinite and a passion that lifts itself heavenward unceasingly. And it is not the child of the sunshine, such a passion; it is the child of mystery and yearning, all which forever cry across this Babylon from the cathedral at our doors.

Might we not illustrate again that effect of vision from the masterpieces of our Christian painting? In ancient Greece and Rome there was but little painting; the art of Athens was the art of sculpture. Now sculpture, whatever else it is, is exquisitely and beautifully clear. Its outline is always perfectly distinct. There is little of awe or mystery in sculpture. And that is why, from the hour that Christ was seen in the infinite reach of His redeeming love, something was wanted of a larger meaning, and the golden age of sculpture was over. Something was wanted to express those longings that are too delicate to be expressed in marble—something that could suggest without defining—that could hint at feelings which never can be uttered, something that does not stand out clear and definite under the sunshine of an Athenian sky but hides as much as it reveals.

Hence sculpture passed and painting came, with its thoughts that wander through eternity, with its remembrance of unutterable agony, with its mystical light upon the face of motherhood. And any man who has once looked on that, and come to it from some piece of ancient statuary, will understand the vision of Isaiah. "In the year that Uzziah died I saw the Lord," and Christendom like him has seen the Lord. She has seen His love, His agony, His beauty, His faith unquenchable in every prodigal. And life can never be the same again, never so clear as in the long ago. There are depths of love in it, and shadows of the cross and a brooding mist from the eternal hills.

Not only is that true of Christendom, but it is true also of the individual soul. I think there are many here who will understand the shadowing that often follows on illumination. Many of us, for instance, have had this experience. We go on living in our daily round, tolerably well contented with ourselves. We have formed our habits, we have settled down, and conscience wearied out has fallen asleep. We remember a time perhaps when it was very different, when we followed the gleam and did it bravely, but it has faded into the light of common day. And then we meet with somebody who has never faltered, who has wrestled heavenward against storm and tide, who has clung through all the stress and strain of years to the ideals which once were ours, and we have lost them. That is an hour of moral and spiritual vision as true as any that Isaiah had, and do not some of you know too well how in that hour the house is filled with smoke? That glimpse of the highest does not bring the sunshine. It brings a dumb unutterable shame. All our careless, prayerless, easy habits—how they rebuke us in such an hour as that.

If that be so when we see some noble life which has clung to the highest through stormy wind and tempest, how much more when we have seen the Lord. The publican saw Him in the temple and cried, "God be merciful to me a sinner" (Luke 18:13). Peter saw Him, and cried out of the depths, "Depart from me, O Lord! I am a sinful man" (Luke 5:8). Job had heard of Him by the hearing of the ear, but when he saw Him he abhorred himself and repented in dust and ashes. In the year that Uzziah died I saw the Lord, and the house was filled with radiance and with song? No, no, not that, thank God—"I saw the Lord, and the house was filled *with smoke*." You understand that now? It has been true of you? Yes, true of Christendom and true of you. It is God's way to character and service. It is the road to the radiance of the morn.

"I sleep, but my heart waketh" (Song of Sol. 5:2).

25
The Higher Ministries of Sleep

When we divide life, as we generally do, into a waking and a sleeping period, we are prone always to exalt the former and to depreciate the latter. That sleep is essential to the body and that for wearied bodies it is a blessed thing, that of course is familiar to us all as one of life's unvarying experiences. But much less familiar is the other thought of the higher and holier offices of sleep, of its moral and religious values. When we think of character we think of action. We recall the stress and struggle of the day. We dwell on the conscious efforts which we make and on the battles with temptation which we fight. And sleep is so utterly diverse from all that and so separate from those struggles which make manhood, that we rarely reckon with it very seriously in the moral and spiritual life.

This point of view is often so exaggerated that sleep is spoken of contemptuously. Men have forgotten that most gracious text, "He giveth his beloved sleep" (Ps. 127:2). All right-thinking people scorn the sluggard, and they scorn him because they *are* right-thinking. "A little slumber—a little sleep—a little folding of the hands to sleep" (Prov. 6:10). The Bible trains its artillery of scorn on the man who wastes his precious hours slothfulness, and conscience is the ally of the Bible. What men have often failed to keep in mind is that

The Higher Ministries of Sleep

the worst is the corruption of the best. They have forgotten that slothfulness is bad just because sleep is good. They have not remembered that every hour of being has its contribution to the higher life, and that the ordering of our existence is of God. How often holy men have spoken of sleep as if it were a thing to be despised. Asceticism has held it in contempt; sainthood has fought against it gallantly. And this superior attitude toward sleep, so often the attitude of cloistered piety, rests on the feeling that for the higher life the hours controlled by sleep are ineffectual. It never seems to have dawned on such ascetics that in so arguing they were arraigning God. It never seems to have occurred to them that they were making themselves wiser than their Maker. If God has given us love, then love is good. If He has given us night, then night is blessed. If He has given the ministry of sleep, then sleep has finer issues than we know.

I remark, in passing, that our Lord seems ever to have felt the mystery of sleep. There were many things contemptible in His eyes, but sleep was never numbered among these. There was one experience of our humanity which moved our Lord down to the very depths. You know from the gospel narrative what that was? It was the dread experience of death. Look at Him beside the grave of Lazarus as He groaned in spirit and was troubled there, and you will feel at once how for Him who is our life there lay an appalling mystery in death. Now the thing to note is that for that dark mystery the word upon the lips of Christ was *sleep*. "Our friend Lazarus sleepeth, but I go to awake him out of sleep" (John 11:11). And that does not mean that death is less mysterious, but it means that sleep is more mysterious for Christ than for the men and women around Him. Love grows more mysterious to me from the moment in which I learn that God is love. God is not less to me, but light is more when I am divinely taught that God is light. And so if sleep upon the lips of Christ could cover all the mystery of death, then sleep for Christ was something darkly wonderful.

One of the greatest revelations made by sleep is the capacity of man for trusting God. "I will both lay me down in peace and sleep, for thou, Lord, only makest me dwell in safety" (Ps. 4:8). Any of you, who like myself have undergone a serious operation, will remember that strange feeling of surrender which preceded the acceptance of the opiate. It was a great adventuring of faith, a desperate commitment of ourselves, a resolute sundering of every cable that bound us to the old familiar life. Every common night we fall asleep we go on a great adventuring like that. Absolutely and unreservedly we entrust ourselves to the keeping of another. We close our eyes, there comes a numbness over us, we pass away from all familiar things, and *so* He giveth His beloved sleep. Beside us in the hour of operation is the calm face of the surgeon whom we trust; and there are nurses there—ministering angels—ready to obey the slightest bidding. But no mortal has ever seen the hand which administers the opiate of sleep, and the angels of the darkness are invisible. We call it *sleep*; it is unconsciousness.

We call it sleep; it is the great adventure. Into the hands of One we never saw we commit the very citadel of being. And that is how, had we but eyes to see it, we are summoned every evening of our lives, from confidence in self which the day ministers to new and utter confidence in God. Faith would be far harder without sleep. Without sleep it would be incredibly hard. Were life one long uninterrupted toil, faith would vanish to the world of angels. But then the night falls, the shadows deepen, and even the giant has to cease his toil. The king, peasant, cardinal and crofter yield themselves up to the arms of the eternal. Every night that work is going on, silently, universally, unconsciously, in the lone cottage, in the lordly palace, in the hovel where there are rags upon the floor. It is God stooping down upon our weariness. It is heaven cradling us to trust. It is the nightly witness to humanity that without faith it cannot live nor die.

Nor is the *quality* of this nightly faith of a character to be despised. For sleep, which may be the greenest of all pastures, is also the last stronghold of the devil. To wander amid the flowers of the meadow does not require a very lively faith. But to storm the citadel where the foe lurks may call for a faith that is heroic. And it is a matter of very old experience that in the shadowy trenches of our sleep sin makes its last and most determined stand. There is a famous passage in St. Augustine's *Confessions* where he gives us his experience of that. He laments that sins which he had long renounced steal back on him unvanquished in his slumber.[1] And Augustine is not the only man who has emerged victorious from the day to find in the quiet night

---

1. See the *Confessions of Augustine*, chap. 30:41.

another agony. Driven from the battlefield of day, sin seeks the battlefield of night. Conquered on the field where will commands, it hurries to the field where will is not. Sin has its onsets, and evil its attacks, and temptation its most cunning ambushes in green meadows where the poppies grow which God had appointed for our peace. "I will both lay me down in peace and sleep, for thou, Lord, only makest me dwell in safety." We do not only trust where angels are. We trust amid the energies of evil. And therefore it is not an easy faith—it is more wonderful than we imagine—when at nightfall and without a fear, we commend ourselves to the Infinite, and sleep.

Another of the higher offices of sleep is the large room it gives to receptivity. It reveals the power of receptivity as nothing else in human life can do. There is not one of us within this church tonight but is familiar with a striking fact—the fact of the moral and the spiritual changes which are wrought by the agency of sleep. There is a world of meaning in that line of Shakespeare—one of the most familiar of all lines—"Sleep that knits up the ravell'd sleave of care."[2] How different are our difficulties in the morning from what they seemed before we went to rest! How overwhelming was our work last night—how it has shrunk today! Some power has been moving in these silent hours, some other reason brooding on our own, reducing everything to true proportion. Difficulties which we could not face at night can be faced and mastered easily in the morning; thoughts which were inextricably twisted sort themselves out into a living pattern; problems which in the evening seemed insoluble so that we flung them from us and retired to sleep, somehow through sleep have ripened to solution.

How many foolish letters have been burned at the imperious command of sleep. In the evening we were resolved to send them; then sleep came, and they were never sent. How many foolish projects have been checked, and how many ruinous resolves dispelled by the mysterious ministry of sleep. Sleep which brings the closing of the eyes brings also the awaking of the heart. Silently it comes—we hear it not—and then as silently it steals away again. And yet we are assured it has been here by the fairy-gifts which it has left, by the vision, the wisdom, and the hope.

Now it is a very wonderful thing, and not less wonderful because

---

2. From *Macbeth*, Act II; sc. 2, by Shakespeare.

so usual, that all these blessings should be given us when we are in a state of receptivity. Here in our western world we are all strenuous. We believe in the divinity of effort. From early morning until the shades of evening we are unceasingly and indefatigably busy. And then comes sleep, and all our toil is over, and for a little season we are no longer busy; yet in these hours when we are doing nothing, we are getting gifts from heaven which are priceless. Every night we are receiving them; every morning we are conscious of them. And we do not speak about them, nor discuss them; we simply go on living and enjoy them. And all the time, insensibly it may be, there is kept alive in man that frame of heart which feels how innumerable are the gifts of heaven which lie beyond the reach of human toil. Were we always laboring—always striving, always endeavoring for noble ends—then the whole universe would be reduced to the things that we could gain by our endeavoring. But lo, there fall on us the shades of evening; we lay us down in peace and sleep, and the universe is larger than we know. We cannot measure it by our endeavor now. It is broader than the grasping of our hand. It is no use attempting to scale heaven by building our Babel on the plain on Shinar. Heaven is other and larger than we knew. It has blessings that we cannot merit. It has gifts that only come when we are still as in the unconsciousness of sleep.

I shall close by noticing one other of the higher offices of sleep. It is its silent and never-ceasing influence in enlarging our thought of human life. When our Savior was a boy at home, He lived in the secluded vale of Nazareth. Around that village in the sheltered valley stretched the green circle of the hills. And one may reverently believe that on these hilltops, where the view was uninterrupted and magnificent, life became a greater thing for Jesus. Down in the valley life was a little thing. There was no far-reaching prospect or expanse. And men awoke and did their daily work, and so, in narrow limits, life went on.

One can conceive how our Savior, when a boy, would steal away to the silence of the hills and find that life was larger than He knew. In some such fashion do we steal away to the mystical mountaintops of sleep, away from our daily work and common round, and from all the speech and tenderness of home. And lo! Upon life there falls a sense of mystery, and we are haunted by untraveled distances, as was the Savior on the hills of Nazareth. Look at that body sleeping on the couch—how still it is. You would think that it was dead. Closed is the eye; silent is the tongue; deaf to the passing footfall is the ear. Yet who can tell what scenes are being enacted with all the intense reality of life behind these exquisite curtains on the eyes? Someone long since dead is speaking there; some child is in the mother's arms again. Someone who is now a thousand miles away is chattering merrily as of yore. The body sleeps; the senses are sealed up; the will has laid aside its power to rule; yet memory and hope and love and fear are living and triumphant in the darkness. I found no elaborate argument on that. I discuss no theory of dreams.

I only desire to make you feel afresh that there is infinite mystery in slumber. I only desire to make you feel afresh how utterly different our life would be if we were always wakeful and were always toiling and if God did not give to His beloved sleep. It is no mere fancy that in every age God has been thought to speak to man in slumber. It is the infinite mystery of heaven in touch with the mystery of life. It is God approaching in these very hours when time and space have vanished from the soul in the enlargement and liberty of sleep. In every one of us there is a haunting sense that we are spiritually greater than we know, a sense of distance and infinity far beyond our toiling and our tears. And how that sense is kept alive by sleep, by the simple common fact of nightly sleep, we shall never know until we waken in the morning when sleep shall be no more.

"The mount called Olivet, which is from Jerusalem a Sabbath day's journey" (Acts 1:12).

26
The Sabbath Day's Journey

A Sabbath day's journey with the Jews was a quite exact and definite expression. It was a journey of about three-quarters of a mile. In the Exodus, you will remember, the tabernacle was in the center of the camp. On every side of it were ranged the tribes of Israel. Well, from the tabernacle to the farthest tent was a distance of about three-quarters of a mile, and *that* was a Sabbath day's journey. Such was the technical import of the word, but like other words it got a vaguer meaning. It came to mean a short and easy journey, a journey such as anyone might take. And it will help us to understand our text and somewhat of the wealth of meaning in it, if we keep that looser significance in mind. I should like to meditate upon the Mount of Olives. I should like to dwell on the associations which have made that little hill forever hallowed. And then I should like to show you what we learn when we remember that the Mount of Olives was but a Sabbath day's journey from Jerusalem.

Think first, then, how the Mount of Olives is associated with loneliness.

As most of you doubtless are aware, though it may not often be present to your thought, the division of our Bible into chapters is a comparatively modern device. In the Greek Testament there are no chapters. Now unquestionably on the whole the division into chapters is a help; yet there are cases where it is not a help but on the contrary obscures the meaning, and one such most unfortunate division bears directly on the Mount of Olives. At the end of the seventh chapter of St. John we read, "Then every man went away to his own house" (John 7:53). At the beginning of the next chapter, "Jesus went to the Mount of Olives." And it is only when we take these two together and let them lie together in the mind that we feel what the writer wanted us to feel, the spiritual loneliness of Christ. Every man went unto his own house: Jesus went unto the Mount of Olives. It haunts the memory, that lonely figure, homeless when all the company went home. And then, deepening the feeling greatly and throwing a light on the loneliness of Christ, we are told here that the Mount of Olives *was but a Sabbath day's journey from Jerusalem.*

Now loneliness is of many kinds, just as love is of many kinds. And there are many pictures of loneliness in Scripture, that perfect mirror of the human heart. There is the loneliness of Cain when he was driven out from the face of living men. There is the loneliness of Abraham when he went out not knowing whither he went. And there is the loneliness of the apostle John when he was an exile on the isle of Patmos where in the evening when the sun was setting, he would sit by the sad waves on the seashore. All these were far away from friends and kindred. They were separated from all the ties of home. Their eyes looked out on unfamiliar scenes where was no form of comrade or of brother.

But the loneliness of Christ was of another kind. It was the loneliness of Olivet, and Olivet was but a Sabbath day's journey from Jerusalem. Not far away from Him were happy homes. He saw the sunshine flashing on the walls. In the still evening He could hear the voices of the children who were playing in the marketplace. His was a loneliness amid familiar scenes and not far distant from familiar faces—where men were toiling, and cottage fires were smoking, and mothers were rocking their little ones to sleep.

Perhaps we more clearly recognize the truth of this when we compare our Savior with the Baptist. The Baptist was a very solitary figure. The Baptist withdrew himself from human fellowship— retired to the solitude of deserts—moved apart from men, far from the markets where the lonely reeds were shaken by the wind. And yet the Baptist, for all his desert-solitude, does not touch one with such a sense of loneliness as Christ who moved among the haunts of men. The one was a recluse and dwelt apart; the other the friend of publicans and sinners. The one was a harsh and rigorous ascetic; the other was infinitely genial. He loved the children, He went to marriages, and He moved in the traffic of the village street; yet I wonder if in all the centuries there has ever been such loneliness as Christ's. The loneliness of John was desert loneliness; it was the loneliness of isolation. But the loneliness of Christ was not like that. His was the loneliness of Olivet.

And is it not the case that loneliness like that is very often the most intense of all? It is not those who are alone who are most lonely.

> There is a pleasure in the pathless woods.
> There is a rapture by the lonely shore.
> There is society where none intrudes,
> By the deep sea, and music in its roar.[1]

But often there is a loneliness unutterable in the crowded city where the streets are thronged, and the windows are brilliantly lighted in the evening. That is the loneliness of every city; it is the loneliness of every Christmas where love and life and sympathy and comradeship may be so near and yet so far away. And that, too, was the loneliness of Olivet where Jesus went when everyone went home, only a Sabbath day's journey from Jerusalem.

In the second place, let us recall how the Mount of Olives is associated with agony. It is there that we find the agony of Christ; you remember the story of that agony? When the supper was ended, they sang a hymn together, and then they went out to the Mount of Olives. They went down to the valley and across the brook and so upward to that place where there was a garden. And there, under the silvery olive trees, with the light of the moon making them beautiful, our Savior was sorrowful even unto death. There He wrestled in spirit with His cross, until His fast-falling sweat was red as blood. There He fought His battle for the crown. There He conquered the

---

1. From "Childe Harold's Pilgrimage" by George Gordon (Lord) Byron (1788–1824).

shrinking of the flesh. And all this anguish, which has redeemed the world, was experienced upon the slope of Olivet only *a Sabbath day's journey from Jerusalem.*

Now as with loneliness, so is it too with agony. There is agony of many kinds in Scripture. There is every sort of human anguish there in that immortal mirror of mortality. There is the agony of Abraham when he climbed Moriah to sacrifice his son. There is the agony of Hagar out in the desert with her little Ishmael.

And you must take such agonies as these and compare them with that under the olive trees to understand the agony of Christ. The agony of Abraham was on the lonely mountain where was never a sound except the calling wind. That of Hagar was in a dreary desert where was never the beating of a heart. But the agony of Christ was in a garden, a garden under the shelter of Mount Olivet, and Olivet was but a Sabbath day's journey from Jerusalem. All that anguish, not on the lonely moor, but known in its bitterness under the olive trees amid familiar scenes where folk were moving, where the bridles rang upon the path and Jerusalem but a little distance off, where mothers watched and little children dreamed, where some were toiling, some were making merry, and some were brokenhearted.

Now does it not occur to you, my hearer, that *that* is an illuminating thought? The greatest and most poignant sufferings—are they not always near the haunts of men? Men fly to the wilderness and suffer there, as many a hermit and anchorite[2] has done. Men scale the snowy cliffs and suffer there, as in heroic adventure on the Alps. Yet perhaps the sorest and most bitter suffering is not the suffering of distant solitudes, but that which (like the Lord Himself) is not far away from any one of us. It is suffering within hail of home and in the midst of the familiar faces. It is the suffering of love despised, of friendship broken, of service unrewarded. It is the suffering of being true to God in daily duty and at every cost; it is the suffering of fatherhood and motherhood. Such agony is not a distant thing; it is not like that of Abraham or Hagar. It is near at hand, amid the lives we cling to, within the sound of voices that we love. It is the anguish not of Mount Moriah where everything was desolate and still. It is the anguish of the Mount of Olives.

---

2. A person who lived a solitary and ascetic life in order to triumph over the flesh in the fourth to fifth centuries A.D.

In the third place, and lastly, I observe that the Mount of Olives is associated with triumph: it was the scene of the Ascension of the Lord. It is not often that farewells are victories; very often they are tragedies. Had we

> Never met or never parted,
> We had ne'er been brokenhearted.[3]

But the farewell of our Lord was not a tragedy; it was the crowning hour of all that He had lived for, "who for the joy set before him, endured the cross, despising the shame" (Heb. 12:2). That hour was the coronation of His work. It was the completion of His career of service. It was the victorious ending of His toil and tears, of His humiliation and His sacrifice. And to me it is beautiful that all this happened, not in some remote and shadowy region, but *within a Sabbath day's journey of Jerusalem.*

Compare, for instance, the going home of Christ with the going home of Moses. One feels the difference between Christ and Moses by a comparison like that. Moses went home upon a lonely height, far from the pleasant stir of human life. It was a desolate and dreary spot where God unlocked the gate and took him in. But Christ went home amid familiar scenes and with the voices of those He loved around him, not far away from the city of His ancestry. The eagle was wheeling and the wind was calling when "God kissed Moses, and he slept." His work was over, his splendid service finished, and the scene was far and desolate and lonely. But the triumph of Christ was of another kind. He went to the liberty of heaven from Olivet, and Olivet—a Sabbath day's journey from Jerusalem.

Now did it ever suggest itself to you, how exquisitely beautiful that was? Christ triumphed then where He has triumphed always, near to the common home and common heart. There is a triumph of the lonely student, keeping his vigil separate from men. There is a triumph of the Arctic traveler when he wins at last the silence of the pole. But every victory that Christ has won has been wrought out where men and women are, amid those hopes and fears and passions and affections which are the warp and woof of all humanity. It is Christ who has transfigured home, the lot of childhood, and the love of motherhood. It is Christ who has ennobled common life,

---

3. From "Ae Fond Kiss" by Robert Burns.

touching it with the glory of the infinite. He has won His victories where He was lonely, found His triumphs where He found His agony, not far away in any voiceless wilderness, but within sound of the voices of the city. That is why we can turn to Him tonight, certain that He is not far away. That is why we can say with glowing hearts, "I triumph still, if thou abide with me." And that, I take it, is why He passed victorious into that heaven where His Father dwells from a familiar little hill called Olivet which is but a Sabbath day's journey from Jerusalem.

"Ye have need of patience" (Heb. 10:36).

27
Patience

There are some virtues which are exclusive virtues and are only demanded in peculiar circumstances. They have at the best a partial application. In certain emergencies they are obligatory or in certain social relationships; that virtue of which we speak tonight can never be included among these. The child needs patience when he goes to school, for without it he will never learn. The boy needs patience on the football field, for without it he will never play. The mother needs it among her growing children; the father, amid the anxieties of business; he who is in work needs it every day, and he who is out of work needs it even more.

There are certain natures, it is true, more liable than others to impatience, and sometimes the finest natures are so tempted. There is a note of impulse and of eagerness in certain natures which are full of charm—a nimbleness of apprehension, a sudden flashing as of a swallow's wing—and often it is natures such as these, which do so much to beautify society, that are most sorely tempted to impatience. It is the fairest of our Highland lakes which are most liable to sudden storm. In a tamer country they would escape the squall; we could reckon on them more in duller levels. But the very grandeur of the hills around them tosses them swiftly into wild commotion, and so is it with certain men and women. We think of

Moses, meekest of God's servants, shattering the tables of the law. We think of Peter in impulsive loyalty cutting off the ear of the priest's servant. And we seem to see the Highland lake again with its silent hills forever reaching heavenward and its corries[1] which are the caverns of the wind.

It is well also to remember constantly that there is a noble and an ignoble patience. Of this, as of all the other virtues, the devil always has his counterfeit. If we seek for the perfect pattern of patience, instinctively we turn to our Redeemer; yet of one thing Christ was utterly impatient, and that one thing was evil. Those fierce denunciations of the Pharisees, that groaning beside the grave of Lazarus are all in the picture of the patient Christ. It is the duty of no one to be patient when evil can be checked or wrong be righted. All our liberties were won for us by heroic impatience of the wrong. There are times when patience is the badge of weakness and ruthlessly betrays the faithless heart; there are times when impatience is divine. Had Robert the Bruce[2] been patient under tyranny, where would our liberty have been today? Had Knox[3] been patient and borne the yoke in meekness, where would have been the church of Christ in Scotland? And had we been patient in this present hour, when the dearest human rights are being imperiled, when nations are being trampled underfoot, when the bond of honor is a scrap of paper, Christ would have said to us, "I never knew you; depart from me, ye cursed of my Father" (Matt. 25:41).

So long as evil is avoidable, every follower of Christ must be impatient of it. It may be criminal to be a martyr when it is possible to be a soldier. No man is worthy to be a Christian citizen or to have place within the Christian commonwealth who cannot be splendidly impatient sometimes with tyranny, cruelty, and evil. My Christian friend, that is *ignoble* patience—shall I tell you what *noble* patience is? Noble patience is the cheerful bearing of what is inevitable and unavoidable. It is in the chastisements sent to you from God; it is in the sufferings which you have to bear; it is in the trials upon the line of duty that "ye have need of patience." Ignoble patience is the child of cowardice. It is afraid "to lose with God." It is the fruitful

---

1. a circular mountain hollow
2. Robert the Bruce (1274–1329), King of Scotland.
3. John Knox (1513–1592), Scottish Protestant Reformer.

mother of injustice, the perpetuator of social abuses. Noble patience welcomes what is sent, believes that behind everything is God, and issues in a quiet which is victory. Matthew Arnold[4] in one of his choicest poems calls patience "the neighbor of despair." But the patience of the Lord Jesus Christ is never the neighbor of despair. It is the neighbor of high and quenchless hope, of confidence that the best is yet to be, of trust in the providence which counts the stars and providentially caters for the sparrow.

Always, too, we should remember that patience is something different from endurance. It is possible to endure and not be patient. Endurance is a very noble virtue; nothing great was ever done without it. There is a world of meaning in our Scottish proverb, *He that tholes, o'ercomes.*[5] But patience in the fullness of its import is ethically finer than endurance; it is endurance with sunshine on its brow. Patience is endurance which is willing. It is endurance with gladness in its mien. It is the endurance which recognizes God and the infinite wisdom of His ordering. It is the endurance which is only possible when one is sure that love is at the helm and that all things work together for his good. A man may endure with curses in his heart. But patience has no curses in its heart. "Let not your heart be troubled, neither let it be afraid" (John 14:27). Patience is endurance in Christ's company, and it takes the cross up with a ready mind for it leans upon the perfect love of God.

Patience is needed in peculiar measure for all development of human character. "In your patience you shall win your souls" (Luke 21:19)—your *selves*. Every person, that is, has a true self, hidden amid the ruins of his or her nature. And as a mother from a burning homestead wins her child, so persons must win their lives. And the only way to do it is the long way, the long and tedious and patient way—in your patience you shall win your souls. Just as there are no shortcuts to heaven, so are there no shortcuts to character. If it takes long to grow a mustard seed, it will take longer still to grow a person. And therefore we have need of patience when we are tempted to what is swift and flashy—tempted to forget that of all lengthy ways there are none so lengthy as the ways of God. "All these kingdoms will I give thee now, if thou wilt fall down and

---

4. Matthew Arnold (1822–1888), English poet and critic.
5. "thole"—endures

worship me" (Matt. 4:9; Luke 4:6–7). It was the great temptation of the Christ as He looked out upon His opening ministry. And then He chose the long and lowly way by the garden of Gethsemane and Calvary and so came to His kingdom and His crown.

Once again, do we not need patience in regard to the plans and purposes of God? "The mills of God grind slowly."[6] Beautiful is the patience of a nurse ministering to some restless invalid; beautiful the patience of a mother among her children who are never still; but in a world like this where night is loth to flee and the crimson morning is so slow in coming, it calls for a patience not less real than that if man is to believe in God. Think of the state of things today. Every hospital is full of wounded men; every city thronged with homeless fugitives; every field in Northern France today has been opened for the burial of the slain.

All this has come after the faith of centuries, mystic communion of the Holy Supper, and praise unceasing from a million tongues to "Jesus, lover of my soul." My Christian hearer, that is hard to bear, and it is harder still to understand. It is as though He who sits in the heavens were making merry with the toil of ages. And what I say is that in this present hour, more than in any hour that we have lived—*we have need of patience.* Patience to believe that with the Lord a thousand years are as one day; to believe that He makes the wrath of man to praise Him and the remainder of His wrath He shall restrain; to believe that He is King of kings, that in His hand there is the heart of princes, that He sees the end from the beginning.

It is not enough, remember, to endure. About our endurance there is no debate. As Britons with a lineage of heroes we shall carry through the task we have begun. But we are more than Britons, we are Christians; we have made our peace with God through Jesus Christ; and as Christians we have need of patience

Endurance says, "I will carry this thing through." Patience says, "God reigns." Endurance says, "Lord, increase my courage." Patience says, "Lord, increase my faith." Endurance says, "Give me the iron will that I may never falter in my calling"; but patience, "Open mine eyes that I may see." That is why at such a time as this there is supreme need of spiritual patience. It is not that the issue may be victory; endurance might be adequate for that. It is that

---

6. Friedrich Von Logan (1604–55), "Sinnged ichte" (1653).

through all gathering of storm-clouds which hang so dark around the throne in heaven, we may walk quietly as men who have a God.

In closing may I ask you to observe how the gospel always has been the friend of patience? It has been so mainly in two ways, and the former is by making love supreme. What is it, tell me, that makes the mother patient amid the worries of her little family? What was it that made Jacob patient when for seven years he served for Rachel? Duty can touch the heart to stern endurance, to scorn delights and live laborious days, but for the finest patience you need love. And now I turn to the old gospel story, and what do I find in the very center there? I find a love sealed in the cross of Christ, a love victorious which will not let us go. It is that love in its infinite benediction falling with power on our fretting hearts which helps us to the patience that we need.

And then, the other secret? The other is the hope of immortality. For a thousand frettings Christ has given patience by bringing immortality to light. There is a splendid saying of St. Augustine's which every one of us should lay to heart. "God is patient," says St. Augustine, "because he is eternal." With all eternity to work His works in, how could the Almighty fret or chafe? And Christ has brought immortality to light. We are no longer the creatures of a day. We do not cease our service at the grave. All we have striven to do and striven to be shall be carried over into the great forever. There is something very quieting in that, something which sheds a gleam on every failure; something which helps us wonderfully in those seasons when above everything we have need of patience.

"After these things, and this faithfulness,
Sennacherib king of Assyria came"
(2 Chron. 32:1, R.V.).

28
Unexpected Issues

There is a note of wonder in these words, an evident feeling of perplexity. The writer is as a man who has been staggered by the mysterious providence of God. Hezekiah was one of the best kings who ever sat upon the throne of Judah. The great ambition of his reign was to reorganize religion in the land. How strenuously he addressed himself to that and how unremittingly he labored at it is told us in the preceding chapters of this book. Other monarchs gave themselves to conquest, Hezekiah to the reformation of religion. Other kings consulted their own interests, Hezekiah the interests of God. For that he labored, and for that he lived; to that he subordinated everything; he was a God-fearing and a pious king. Now to the Jew, more than to other men, one result to such conduct seemed inevitable. God would remember godly Hezekiah and would bless him with prosperity and peace. And the perplexing thing for pious souls, the thing which they found it hard to understand, was that *after these things Sennacherib came.* After that life of strenuous endeavor, after these years of loyalty to heaven, after that noble effort at reform which was the glory of Hezekiah's reign, the Assyrian came down like a wolf on the fold. It is no wonder the writer was perplexed and the godly utterly confounded. It was as if the promises of heaven were shattered into fragments. Men could not understand the meaning of it nor fathom the mystery of such a providence, when after these things and that faithfulness, Sennacherib king of Assyria came.

Yet when we meditate on human life, such an outcome does not seem exceptional; it is a common ordering of God. Only a week ago, for instance, we sat together at the communion table. It was a blessed hour of spiritual fellowship, and the banner over us was love. We felt as if heaven were not far away, as if Jesus of Nazareth were passing by, so conscious were we of the redeeming presence. What memories of the past awoke within us; what golden hopes of discipleship to be; what vows were registered—what prayers went heavenward—what petitions for the coming days! And after all these things Sennacherib came. Some perhaps had hardly left the table when the most terrible anxieties beset them. I know of one who found on reaching home that things would never be the same again. And some on Monday were so sorely tempted with the very temptations they had prayed against, that it seemed as if God had forgotten to be gracious. After these things Sennacherib came—after the joy and sweetness of the supper; after the dedication to the covenant-God of body, soul, and spirit—not peace but all the bitterness of struggle; not prosperity but rude awakening; not feet that were beautiful upon the mountains but the horrid pit and miry clay.

That experience of the Lord's Supper is also repeated at the close of years. It is frequent in the biographies of Scripture. I think of Abraham in heroic loyalty leaving everything to follow God; he has hardly settled in the land of Canaan before there is a famine in the land. I think of Job, perfect before God, reverent and righteous and blameless, and then the blast of the whirlwind on his flocks and the Chaldeans carrying off his children. I think of one who lay on Jesus' bosom, of the disciple whom He loved, one who knew Him as none other knew Him and was admitted to His closest intimacy—after these things and that faithfulness, an exile upon the isle of Patmos. Why should Abraham have been treated so? Why should that banishment have been the fate of John? Why should men and women after years of faithfulness be called to suffer terribly? That was what perplexed the chronicler and has perplexed a thousand hearts since then in the darkening shadows that follow years of loyalty. I had a call the other day from a dear friend who has long been a minister of Christ. Now he is ill, and as he sat and talked with me he coughed, and there was lung-blood in the cough. And he said to me with that brave smile of his, "It seems an unheroic ending, does it not?"—and I answered, *After these things Sennacherib came.* Then I thought of that imperial statesman[1] who was smitten down in the prime of his activities. I thought of one who dwelt beside the Tweed,[2] when his hand trembled and the shadows fell. And it seemed to me that the chronicler's perplexity was the perplexity of all the ages in the face of the baffling providence of God.

One often lights on a similar experience in the high activities of Christian service. It may be the service of a mother; it may be that of a teacher or a friend. I have known a teacher give herself for years to the redemption of a single girl. She has befriended her unceasingly. She has prayed for her every night and every morning. She has done all that woman's wit could do to shield her in the hour of temptation, and after all these things Sennacherib came. Just when the golden circle was complete, came the temptation which rent it into fragments. Just when the palace was rising to its copestone, came the blast, and it was all in ruin. Just when the efforts were on the verge of crowning, and when prayers had multiplied before the throne of God, the Assyrian, like a wolf, was on the fold.

I wonder if this text was in the mind of Jesus on that night when Simon Peter fell. How He had toiled for Peter, how He had lived for Peter, how He had prayed for Peter that his faith fail not. And after these things and that faithfulness, staunch and real through many a dreary day—after all these things Sennacherib came. If I am speaking to any mother here who is tempted to think that God has quite forgotten her, to any teacher of a mission-class who is tempted to think her labor is in vain, I want her to remember that in every age that has been the perplexity of faith, and yet tonight people are still trusting God.

Nor at such an hour as this can we forget that that is also a national experience. It was the cry of the king of Judah long ago; it is the cry of the king of Belgium tonight.[3] I do not say—it

---

1. Possibly William Pitt the Younger (1759–1806), English politician whose premature death occasioned great regret in Britain.

2. The river Tweed in southeast Scotland.

3. Preached when offerings were being taken for Belgian refugees during World War I.

would be false to say—that Belgium has been a religious country. But I do say, and say with all my heart, that Belgium has been a faithful country—faithful to the thought of duty, faithful to the life of labor, faithful to the ideal of liberty. Set in the midst of great and envious nations she has pursued her task with fine fidelity; she has troubled nobody—interfered with nobody—coveted the territory of nobody.

She has built her cities and multiplied her looms and enriched her fields and educated her children. She has given the kindliest welcome to the stranger. That is not great nor glorious, it may be; but it is better than glorious, it is faithful. Of Belgium might it be said with perfect truth, "Well done, thou faithful servant." And now the baffling mystery is this—and it must have torn with anguish many a heart—that after these things and that faithfulness, Sennacherib came. It is the ancient story in the modern world. That is the thought I want you to remember. It is not a difficulty of our yesterday; it has been the problem of the ages. And if in the face of it right down the centuries people have maintained a living trust in God, be not recreant,[4] friends, to your heritage. We are so apt to think our problem is exceptional and our experience without a parallel; so apt to think our faith in God is tried as the faith of God's people was never tried before. I plead for a larger view than that tonight. I want you to take the verdict of the ages. With God's own people thousands of years ago, after that faithfulness it was the same.

And just to show you that such perplexing issues must have their meaning in the love of God, I want you to remember Christ; for if anything be true of Christ, it will be true of the race He represents. If ever there was a life supremely faithful, it was the life of Jesus. Never, never by a single thought did He swerve from perfect loyalty to God. In the smallest matters of His daily conduct as in the mightiest service of His ministry, He was unfalteringly and passionately true. Talk of the fellowship of a communion season—the life of Jesus was an unbroken fellowship. He saw God everywhere and walked with Him; He served Him with a love that never wavered.

Then after a life like that, so full and flawless in its filial confidence—the betrayal and the garden and the cross. After these things

---

4. false

Sennacherib came: after His prayers upon the mountainside; after an hour when He had fed the multitudes and had called to the winds and waves and they obeyed Him; after an hour when He had raised the dead; and after another hour in which He was transfigured. Moses and Elias talked with Him, and His garments were as lustrous as the sun. After all that perfect faithfulness you would not look for the garden of Gethsemane. And after the faithfulness, of Hezekiah you would not look for the army of Sennacherib. And it helps one's faith just to remember that God loved Christ with all a Father's love, and yet He too experienced that issue.

I close by asking whether in our passage any light is cast upon that mystery? Must we just bow the head and trust, or is there any gleam upon the cloud? Two thoughts at once arise.

The first is that this strange issue cast Hezekiah utterly on God. Read through the chapter carefully, and you find a steady deepening of dependence. At first, when the news of the invasion came, Hezekiah acted like a courageous king. He marshaled his armies, set everything in order, heartened his men for battle. And then the darkness deepened, and Hezekiah *cried unto the Lord*. Probably from the outset he had prayed. Perhaps at the first, prayer had been secondary. Now he recognized the grim reality that without God everything was lost. And so Sennacherib did more for him than all his busy adornment of the temple, for he drove him to the arm of the Almighty. After these things Sennacherib came—

> Abide with me; fast falls the eventide;
> When other helpers fail, and comforts flee,
> Help of the helpless, O abide with me.[5]

How often God so uses our Sennacherib to cast us on the eternal arm—to make us feel that without Him we are lost.

And then God used this coming of Sennacherib to show the greatness of His delivering power. Man's extremity was God's opportunity. What happened to the Assyrian army the Bible tells us in the most guarded way. Was it some pestilence that fell on it? Was it some panic fear? All we are told is that an angel smote it, the mighty host became a broken rabble, and Sennacherib was murdered by his

---

5. "Abide with Me" by Henry F. Lyle (1793–1847).

sons. After all these things Sennacherib came, came in pride, went home again in ruin—came to destroy, went home again destroyed, a broken and a shattered emperor.

Judah saw it and rejoiced in God, and Hezekiah sang the psalm of Israel, "Thou hast an arm that's full of power, Thy hand is great in might" (Ps. 89:13). My Christian friend, if I am not mistaken, history is going to repeat itself. The day is coming when in this very sanctuary you and I are going to sing that psalm. Meantime, through the darkest day let us do our duty in quiet trust in God, remembering how, hundreds of years ago, *after these things came Sennacherib.*

"The sea is his, and he made it" (Ps. 95:5).

29
The Ministry of the Sea

One of the lessons of our modern knowledge is the littleness of the world in which we dwell. It is no longer a stupendous sphere; it is relatively a tiny habitation. There was a time when humans conceived our world to be the center of the created universe. The sun arose simply to give it light, and the stars were flung abroad to be its ornaments. But now by the ruthless hand of exact science our earth has been displaced from that centrality, and we are the tenants of a tiny planet.

Well now, this little planet—what do we call it? We say it is our earth. That is just as if we spoke of Lanarkshire,[1] when what we really meant to say was Scotland. For of all the surface of this globe of ours to which we cling so passionately and which we call our earth, four-fifths at least is covered by the sea. Now if "God formed the world to be inhabited" (Isa. 45:18), that is a fact of most profound significance. God formed this world to be inhabited by making more than three-quarters of it uninhabitable. For every man who really believes in the divine significance of things, that is a fact which merits consideration.

Of course, the contrast between land and sea is not so perfect as

---

1. County Lanark in Scotland.

we at first conceive. We recognize that in our common speech when we talk of the harvest of the sea. When we look out over the miles of water or when we listen to the surf upon the shore, the first thought to creep into the mind is that of nakedness and loneliness. And we have always to correct that first impression by other thoughts which follow in its train, as of the millions who live upon the sea, and of the mighty revenues which are derived from it. In spite of all that, the contrast is a real one which no after-thinking can dispel, the contrast between that waste of waters and the orchard and the meadow and the glen; between the bosom of the eager earth responding to the magic touch of summer and the sea that never thrilled to any spring. What does it mean in its divine intention?

The first fact which swims into our ken[2] is one that might be enlarged upon indefinitely: it is the mighty influence which the sea has exercised on the civilization of mankind. God has enlisted many varied instruments in lifting His wistful children out of savagery. He has helped them upon the upward road by the mountain and the river and the moor. But it is questionable if among all His instruments, used with a patience of skill that is divine, there has been any quite so mighty as the sea. Have you ever thought why in a heathen continent things get darker and darker toward the center? The farther you pierce into the heart of Africa, the more inveterate and awful is the savagery. The farther you go from the engirdling ocean with its unceasing and mysterious ministries, the farther you travel from liberty and light. On the great rolling steppes of Central Asia thousands of years ago there roamed the Scythians. And on these rolling steppes this very evening their Tartar children are bivouacking still; unchanged, after the passing of the centuries; uninspired by any loftier calling; uninfluenced by the progress of humanity; untouched by the message of the sea. We talk of the sea as that which divides the world when it is really the sea which binds the world. It is the moor, the desert, the ravine—it is the shaggy mountain which is the real divider. But then there comes a galleon to the harbor, laden with merchandise of faraway, and that one galleon may set a spirit working which will issue in spiritual sunrise by and by. That is why well-nigh every great metropolis has been set in close connection with the sea. Tyre and Carthage; Athens,

---

2. knowledge or perception

Venice, London have all stretched out their hand toward the ocean. And it is in them that commerce has grown kingly, literature has clothed itself in immortality, and art has rejoiced and blossomed as the rose.

The second fact to which I call attention is equally notable and demonstrable; it is the sway which the sea has always exercised over the imagination of mankind. It was Horace Bushnell,[3] if I remember rightly, who said a beautiful thing about the imagination. He said that God gave man imagination that He might have a door to enter by. And all of you will agree with me in thinking that life would be a very barren thing without Him who enters by that door.

Now have you ever thought what stirs imagination, what opens wide those ivory gates and golden? Have you ever thought why many a thing of beauty leaves the imagination cold and dead? I take it that the reason is just this, that in such beauty, though sensuously perfect, there is no presence of the element of mystery. Give me the most exquisite of features, and without soul behind them they shall never haunt me; kindle them with the mystery of spirit, and they appeal to the imagination instantly. Without the haunting of what we cannot fathom, without the suggestion of what we cannot penetrate, the imagination never is awakened. That is why Christianity so powerfully has quickened the imagination of mankind. It is because at the heart of all its beauty there lies forever that element of mystery. And that is why the vision of the sea has profoundly influenced imagination also; it is so beautiful and so mysterious.

There was a time when the land was full of mystery. That time is swiftly drawing to an end. You can travel to Damascus in the train now; you can send a wire from the Clyde to the ends of the earth. The mystery of the broad earth is vanishing before the inroad of railway and of telegraph, and the last great home of mystery is the sea. Think of all its mystery of distance; think of all its mystery of depth. Think of the thousand secrets that are shrouded where the *Lusitania* lies moldering tonight. To me, in all the range of literature, there is nothing more solemnizing than that sentence—*until the sea gives up its dead* (Rev. 20:13).

But not only has the sea through all the ages quickened the imagination of mankind. It has had the task bestowed on it from

---

3. Horace Bushnell (1802–1876), American clergyman and theologian.

heaven of evoking heroic qualities of character. It has been the noble office of the hills to quicken and sustain the love of liberty. It has been the duty of the valleys to foster the gift of melody and song. And it has been one great ministry of level land to foster that humble, patient, quiet labor, lacking which no land is ever wealthy and never a harvest ripens in the sun. God has His work for hill and plain to do. God has His work for every smiling valley. And "the sea also is his, and he hath made it" (Ps. 95:5), shall it not also have its appointed office? I think that unquestionably it has had that office and has been exercising it through all the centuries in calling out the heroic in humanity. What heroes the first navigators were! Did you ever think of their heroic daring? There were no charts for them—no lighthouses—no sound of bell on any sunken reef. And yet, like Peter on the Sea of Galilee, they heard the call, "Launch out into the deep" (Luke 5:4); and hearing it, like Peter, they obeyed.

Keats[4] talks somewhere of "perilous seas forlorn." There was a time when every sea was that; a time when no man knew, driving before the wind, if he were making for El Dorado[5] or Charybdis[6]. And yet I see the tiny, fragile vessels faring forth into a world of waters; behind them is all the sunshine on the grass, the voices of children, and the peace of home. Sweet to mortal is the summer sunshine—sweet is the languorous shimmering on the vine—sweet is the laughter of the little child and the crooning of the mother in the home; but in a world like this where everything is difficult, there is needed another and more heroic message, and what I say is that that heroic message has ever been the message of the sea. It has turned the faces of men to the unknown. It has roused the spirit of heroic daring. It has given the faculty of swift response in the presence of unexpected difficulties. It has contributed to human character what the lilies of the field could never give. The sea also is His, and He has made it.

There is one other message of the sea which it is fitting we should mention here. It is that it has helped to keep alive in every age the sense of the grandeur and the majesty of God. It has some-

---

4. From "Sonnet: On the Sea" by John Keats (1785–1821), English poet.
5. Legendary treasure city in South America.
6. Mythic whirlpool in the Strait of Messina, NE of Sicily.

times been charged against our Christian faith that it dims the thought of the majesty of God. We do not address Him as the great Creator; we address Him as our Father. We take the most intimate of all relationships with the beautiful sunshine of the home upon it, and we use that of God. Have you not sometimes felt in the prayers of men and women a certain jarring as of familiarity? Have you never been conscious in your own prayers that the thought of the awfulness of God was lacking?

Whenever we are tempted to forget that, in the hurry and fever of activity, God provides us with two mighty spectacles which silently bring it to the heart again. The one is the sky, the silent, starry sky. The other is the sea. The one is far away and inaccessible. The other is washing at our feet. Yet both are so vast that they suggest infinity, so filled with power that we feel our helplessness, so still sometimes upon a summer evening that for us beyond these voices there is peace. I turn to the thousand lilies of the field, and they speak of the exquisite providence of God. I turn to the meadow under the apple trees, and it whispers to my heart that God is love. I turn to the ocean with its infinite distances, within whose depths are hid a million secrets, and I feel that He whom we have known in Christ is sovereign and of majesty unsearchable. You must never lose that sense in any ecstasy. Amid all the pressure of life you must sustain it. It tranquilizes; it allays the fret and fever; it brings the angel-faces back again. And if this summer, for a week or two you are to have your dwelling by the sea, will you listen sometimes for that message?

I close with a simple practical thought, though one which may not have occurred to you. It springs from something of which the scholars tell us in the attitude of Israel to the sea. You and I love the sea, as did the Greeks; but the Jews were different from us and from the Greeks. They looked on the sea with an intense abhorrence just as they looked upon the desert. There is a Jewish proverb to the effect that there are two doors into Gehenna, the one from the desert and the other from the sea. The strange thing is that though they feared it so, they could yet write, *Thy paths are in the sea* (Ps. 77:19). The strange thing is that they had faith to say, "The sea also is his, and he hath made it." That very element which they abhorred and looked upon with vague and shuddering fear reechoed with the footsteps of their God. Is there anything in your life which you abhor—anything of which you are afraid? When you put the shell to your ear in quiet night, is there any sound of dreaded waters in it? I want you to rise to that victorious faith which can look out over a waste of waters and say (what we all can say about the lilies), "The sea also is his, and he hath made it."

"Then lifted I up mine eyes, and saw, and behold four horns" (Zech. 1:18).

30
The Second Vision

The first thing to arrest us in this text is how a second vision followed on the first. *Then*—when he had had one glorious vision—the prophet lifted up his eyes again. Zechariah, despondent, sick at heart, had gone out one evening from the ruined city. He had gone out to pray in some secluded glen where in the hollows the myrtle bushes grew. And there, as he wrestled with heaven in the darkness, God flashed a glory of light upon his soul, such light as never was on sea or land. Zechariah had a glorious vision such as might have contented any man. He saw squadrons of angelic horses; he heard the voice of the angel of the Lord. And then the darkness fell, the angel vanished, the serried chivalry[1] of heaven faded, and Zechariah was left alone again with the night wind and the myrtles in the valley. How many men would have said, "It is enough. Let me steal home again; I have seen everything." The point to note is that the inspired prophet adopted no such final attitude. If he had seen once, he would see again, though heaven was wrapped in impenetrable darkness: "Then lifted I up mine eyes, and saw."

A somewhat similar outlook and expectancy is to be witnessed in

---
1. ranks of horsemen

the apostle Paul. He also knew what Meredith[2] describes as the rapture of the forward view. Like Zechariah, Paul had had his vision. A glory brighter than the sun had flashed on him. He had seen what was better than angelic cavalry: he had seen the risen and glorified Redeemer. And then on him, too, as on Zechariah, there had fallen a darkness fathomless as midnight, and they led him by the hand into the city. How many men would have said, "It is enough: I have seen everything that soul can see." The point to note is that his heroic heart never dreamed of saying such a thing. "Now I know in part and see in part." If he has seen once, he will see again. Then, when the first vision had departed, Paul lifted up his eyes and saw.

The temptation to be content with a first vision is often felt in Christian experience. It is sometimes seen in very striking fashion when people have been suddenly converted. The great majority of Christians nowadays have never consciously experienced sudden conversion. Baptized in infancy and trained in Christian homes, they have never known a time when Christ was not their friend. But there are others here—some of them known to me—who can point back to one decisive moment when old things passed away from them, and all things became new. In such an hour a person is like Zechariah: the heavens are opened above the myrtle bushes. He has come out from a city that is ruined, and everything becomes different in a twinkling. And my point is that if the person be wise he will not think he has exhausted heaven, but steadily and quietly and humbly he will lift up his eyes again and see. There is so much to learn yet of the grace of Christ, such a wealth of experience which only years can bring.

Even Paul, who had seen the living Lord, said, "Now we know in part and see in part" (1 Cor. 13:12). And that is just what Christian experience is: the lifting up of the eyes to other visions which God who gave the first will also give to interpret and to complete the first. Some will come through study of the Bible. Some will come through miserable failure. Some will come to a man when duty calls; some when the beast is straining at the leash. Then, says the prophet in the myrtle valley when the first splendor of heaven had departed, then "I lifted up my eyes and saw."

The next thing which I want you to observe is how the second vision differed from the first. "Then lifted I up mine eyes and saw

---

2. George Meredith (1828–1909), English novelist and poet.

four horns." Now recall what the first vision was. It was a vision of squadrons of angelic horsemen. It was a vision to stir the heart and thrill the spirit, those companies of the cavalry of heaven. The breath of the wide world was in it all. The horsemen had been abroad over the earth, and now they were ranked in squadrons in the valley. It was a splendid vision, full of glory, rich in the pomp and pageantry of war. It was a vision of color and of champing steeds with the echoing note of the bugle in the glen. And then, says the prophet, I lifted up mine eyes, filled with the heavenly splendor of that sight, and I saw, and behold *four horns*. Two oxen, browsing in the rank undergrowth, and tossing their heads now and then as oxen do; and every time they tossed them above the myrtle bushes, four horns appearing for an instant. And you have got to contrast that lowly vision with the splendor of that which immediately preceded it if you would catch the import of it all. The first was wonderful, the second commonplace. The first was magnificent, the second lowly. The first was rich in the pageantry of battle, the second was reminiscent of the village. The first was a vision of infinite horizon, broad as the world and thrilling as a trumpet, and in the second there is the crofter's field and "the lowing herd wind slowly o'er the lea.

And then when you come to meditate a little, you find that this is often heaven's sequence. We all begin with the color and the music, and most of us come to the vision of the horns. I think of youth with its romantic ardor settling down to the tasks of middle age. I think of genius with its flash and insight, and then the weary drudgery that follows. I think of love with its music in the glen and its hopes that are broad as the world and high as heaven, and then of the patient and unexciting service which always follows when love is in the home.

Tell me, did you ever know a child who was going to settle down into a clerk? Are they not all going to be pirate captains, explorers, or generals of armies? And so the years go by and wisdom comes, and in the ordering of God the vision changes, and lo, the cavalry of heaven has vanished, and the quiet oxen are feeding in the valley. Something has touched the children as from heaven to the fine issues of ordinary labor. Once they were eager for a high renown, and now they are thankful for a livelihood. Once, like Zechariah in the glen, they saw the splendid cavalry of angels, and now, a little wiser than in

---

3. Thomas Gray (1716-1771) "Elergy Written in a Country Churchyard."

childhood, they have the lowly vision of four horns. Men talk as if heaven's visions were all golden. But all the visions of heaven are not golden. God has His visions that are clad in gold. He has also His visions that are clad in gray—gray days that have none of the melodies of June; gray tasks that are not shot with any beauty; gray lives that make us sometimes very pitiful. Then lifted I up mine eyes and saw four *cherubim*? Then lifted I up mine eyes and saw four *horns*. A vision of splendid, winged, glorious creatures? A vision of patient, unromantic oxen. My friend of middle age, get to your life again, lift up your eyes and find that God is there, not less than when among the myrtles in the glen there was the shrilling bugle-note of chivalry.

And then the third point I want to note is this, that both these visions were given in one place, in the glen of the myrtles just outside Jerusalem where Zechariah would often go for prayer. Whether both were given in one night it may be impossible for us to say. It is also impossible to say with certainty the exact form the revelation took. But the one point on which there is no doubt and which was unquestionably meant for our instruction is that both the visions were given in the same place. Moses saw God at the burning bush; then the scene changed and he saw God at Sinai. Paul saw Christ on the highway to Damascus; then the scene changed and he saw Christ in prison. But Zechariah in the glen of myrtles had his first vision of the angelic armies; then in that same spot he saw the horns. The meaning is that where he saw the highest, there and nowhere else he saw the lowliest. In the very place where flashed the heavenly steeds browsed the patient, unromantic oxen. He had a vision that thrilled him to the depths, and then a vision of uncomplaining service; both alike were given in the valley.

Now it is a very gracious thing that visions should have different localities. It tells us that we shall not lose the gleam when we leave home and journey far away. But the lesson which Zechariah teaches is a lesson also we do well to learn, that the highest and the lowliest are akin. When I think of the Bible with its heavenly glory and find there also my dull and daily duty, when I discover that no place is fairer than where I do my humble task in loyalty, then do I understand that single glen with its angelic horsemen and its horns.

So do I turn from the prophet to the Christ and find in Him the unity made perfect. "Art thou a king then? Thou sayest I am a king" (John 18:37). "I am the resurrection and the life" (John 11:25). And yet in that same life, aglow with heaven, what vision of common toil and human tears, for He carried our sicknesses and bore our burdens. He who has seen the Lord has seen all chivalry; he has seen something more divine than chivalry. He who has seen the Lord has seen the horns, the vision of what is meek and lowly. And he has seen them both in one lone valley, as Zechariah did outside Jerusalem when he went apart among the myrtle bushes to commune with his own heart and be still.

Scripture Index

GENESIS
16:13 122
37:19 107

EXODUS
20:5 57

DEUTERONOMY
7:25 136

1 SAMUEL
18:7 58

2 KINGS
6:17 52

2 CHRONICLES
32:1 169

NEHEMIAH
4:15 130

PSALMS
4:8 153
8:4 94
32:8 122
46:10 115
73:26 23
77:3 148
77:19 179
89:13 174
95:5 ..175, 178
109:18 46
119:18 48
127:2 152
138:8 70
139:8 120

PROVERBS
6:10 152
15:17 63

ECCLESIASTES
9:10 116

SONG OF SOLOMON
5:2 152

ISAIAH
6:1, 4 147
42:3 106
45:18 175

JEREMIAH
5:10 34

EZEKIEL
2:1 78

ZECHARIAH
1:18 181
2:1–2 74
2:8 62

MATTHEW
3:37 107
4:9 167
4:11 87
5:29–30 ..140
6:9 104
8:20 101
11:27 61
11:29 141
11:35 125
12:49 24
14:30 40
18:3 49
18:4 145
21:5 79
25:21 135
25:41 165
26:50 106
26:52–53 ..89

Mark
4:24 109
8:33 10

Luke
2:14 86
2:49 108
4:6–7 167
4:8 88
5:4 178
5:8 ...33, 151
8:55 133
9:58 101
18:13 ..56, 144, 151
19:41 125
21:19 166
22:42 146
23:34 146

John
1:18 98
1:46 58
2:4 24
5:22 60
7:28, 33 ..146
7:53 159
11:11 153
11:16 25
11:25 184
11:35 125
12:28 111
14:2 99
14:6 60
14:27 166
18:37 184
21:15–17 ..30

Acts
1:12 158
9:8 52
12:16 69
16:25 17
17:23 91

Romans
7:24 67

1 Corinthians
2:9 99
13:1, 3 71
13:11 102
13:12 ..92, 98, 182

2 Corinthians
5:17 49

Galatians
2:20 127

Philippians
1:23 100
3:7 38
4:11 67

2 Timothy
1:12 97

Hebrews
4:15 107
10:36 164
11:1 98
12:2 162
12:22, 24 ..85

1 John
3:2 ...98, 101
3:20 29
4:14 103

Revelation
1:17 92
20:13 177

Additional Sermon Resources

Great Women of the Bible   **Clarence E. Macartney**
A collection of sermons from a master pulpiteer of yesterday. Macartney's unique descriptive style brings these women of the Bible to life and provides inspirational reading for all Christians.

ISBN 0-8254-3268-5   **208 pp.**   **paperback**

The Greatest Questions of the Bible and of Life   **Clarence Edward Macartney**
Discussing such questions as What shall I do with Jesus?, What must I do to be saved?, If a man dies, shall he live again?, and Barabbas or Jesus?, Clarence E. Macartney challenges his readers to ask questions and seek the answers from the pages of Holy Scripture and employ this method of teaching in his or her own situation to great profit.

ISBN 0-8254-3273-1   **192 pp.**   **paperback**

Greatest Texts of the Bible   **Clarence E. Macartney**
This collection of sermons represents some of the author's strongest and most impassioned preaching. Except for slight modifications and updating, and the insertion of Scripture references where needed, these sermons are reissued in their original form.

ISBN 0-8254-3266-9   **208 pp.**   **paperback**

The Greatest Words in the Bible and in Human Speech   **Clarence Edward Macartney**
A group of fifteen sermons based on fifteen words from men's speech and their corresponding biblical meaning and significance. Macartney explores such words as: Sin, Forgiveness, Now, Whisperer, Tomorrow, Why, Repent, Heaven, Memory, Prayer, Death and Experience.

ISBN 0-8254-3271-5   **192 pp.**   **paperback**

He Chose Twelve   **Clarence E. Macartney**
This careful study of the New Testament illuminates the personality and individuality of each of the Twelve Disciples. A carefully crafted series of Bible character sketches including chapters on all the apostles as well as Paul and John the Baptist.
ISBN 0-8254-3270-7   **176 pp.**   **paperback**

Paul the Man   **Clarence E. Macartney**
Macartney delves deeply into Paul's background and heritage, helping twentieth-century Christians understand what made him the pivotal figure of New Testament history. Paul, the missionary and theologian, are carefully traced in this insightful work.
ISBN 0-8254-3269-3   **208 pp.**   **paperback**

Twelve Great Questions About Christ   **Clarence E. Macartney**
Macartney addresses commonly asked questions about the life and person of Jesus Christ. The integrity of the Scriptures underlies the provocative answers that Dr. Macartney provides in this thoughtful book. The broad range of subject matter will inform and inspire laymen and clergy alike as they peruse these pages.
ISBN 0-8254-3267-7   **160 pp.**   **paperback**

Treasury of the World's Great Sermons   **Warren W. Wiersbe**
These outstanding sermons are presented from 122 of the greatest preachers. A short biographical sketch of every preacher is also included. Complete with an index of texts and of sermons. 672 double-column pp.
ISBN 0-8254-4002-5   **672 pp.**   **paperback**

Classic Sermons on the Attributes of God   **Warren W. Wiersbe**
These classic sermons lay a solid foundation for the study of God's attributes such as truth, holiness, sovereignty, omnipresence, immutability, and love. Includes messages by Henry Ward Beecher, J.D. Jones, J.H. Jowett, D.L. Moody, John Wesley, and others.
ISBN 0-8254-4038-6   **160 pp.**   **paperback**

Classic Sermons on the Birth of Christ   **Warren W. Wiersbe**
The central theme of the Bible is expanded and expounded in this collection of sermons from such great preachers as Henry P. Liddon, Walter A. Maier, G. Campbell Morgan, Arthur T. Pierson, James S. Stewart and others.
ISBN 0-8254-4044-0   **160 pp.**   **paperback**

Classic Sermons on Christian Service   **Warren W. Wiersbe**
Dynamic principles for Christian service will be found in these classic sermons by highly acclaimed pulpit masters. Warren W. Wiersbe has carefully selected sermons which describe the essential characteristics of Christian servanthood.
ISBN 0-8254-4041-6   **160 pp.**   **paperback**

Classic Sermons on the Cross of Christ   **Warren W. Wiersbe**
An inspiring collection of sermons on perhaps the most significant event the world ever experienced—the cross of Christ. Through masterful sermons by great pulpit masters, the reader will gain a greater understanding of the theological, devotional, and practical importance of the Cross of Christ.
ISBN 0-8254-4040-8   **160 pp.**   **paperback**

Classic Sermons on Faith and Doubt   Warren W. Wiersbe
A collection of 12 carefully selected sermons, the goal of which is to stimulate the growth and maturity of the believer's faith. Among the preachers represented are: A. C. Dixon, J. H. Jowett, D. Martyn Lloyd-Jones, G. Campbell Morgan, and Martin Luther.
ISBN 0-8254-4028-9   **160 pp.**   **paperback**

Classic Sermons on Family and Home   Warren W. Wiersbe
The erosion of traditional family and biblical values is accelerating at an alarming rate. Dr. Wiersbe has compiled *Classic Sermons on Family and Home* to help recapture God's enduring truth for the family today.
ISBN 0-8254-4054-8   **160 pp.**   **paperback**

Classic Sermons on Hope   Warren W. Wiersbe
Crime. Poverty. Disease. War. Social upheaval. Ecological disaster. Warren W. Wiersbe has chosen twelve classic sermons on hope that will encourage the reader to face struggles with a confident Christian hope. Included are sermons by G. Campbell Morgan, D.L. Moody, Charles Haddon Spurgeon, and A.W. Tozer. Excellent "starter" material for sermon preparation; solid spiritual content for devotional readers.
0-8254-4045-9   **160 pp.**   **paperback**

Classic Sermons on the Names of God   Warren W. Wiersbe
Any study of the names of God in Scripture will be enhanced by the classic sermons included in this collection. They feature sermons from Charles H. Spurgeon, G. Campbell Morgan, John Ker, George Morrison, Alexander MacLaren and George Whitefield.
ISBN 0-8254-4052-1   **160 pp.**   **paperback**

Classic Sermons on Overcoming Fear   Warren W. Wiersbe
Classic sermons by such famous preachers as Alexander Maclaren, V. Raymond Edman, Clarence Macartney, George H. Morrison, Charles H. Spurgeon, George W. Truett and others. Wiersbe has chosen sermons which offer insight as well as hope for believers faced with the uncertainty of this pilgrim journey.
ISBN 0-8254-4043-2   **160 pp.**   **paperback**

Classic Sermons on Prayer   Warren W. Wiersbe
Fourteen pulpit giants present the need for and the results of a life permeated with prayer. These sermons by such famous preachers as Dwight L. Moody, G. Campbell Morgan, Charles H. Spurgeon, Reuben A. Torrey, Alexander Whyte, and others, will help you experience the strength and power of God in prayer.
ISBN 0-8254-4029-7   **160 pp.**   **paperback**

Classic Sermons on the Prodigal Son   Warren W. Wiersbe
These sermons by highly acclaimed pulpit masters offer unique insights into perhaps the most famous of Christ's parables. These sermons will provide new understanding of the relationships between the son, father and other son. Believers will also be challenged to apply the wonderful truth of the Father's love to their own lives. .
ISBN 0-8254-4039-4   **160 pp.**   **paperback**

Classic Sermons on the Resurrection of Christ   Warren W. Wiersbe
These sermons represent the best in scholarship, warmed by deep inspiration and enlivened by excitement about what the Resurrection of Christ means to the believer.
ISBN 0-8254-4042-4   **160 pp.**   **paperback**

Classic Sermons on the Second Coming
and other Prophetic themes **Warren W. Wiersbe**
The second coming of Christ is a promise presented in many New Testament passages. Dr. Wiersbe has marshaled an array of classic sermons on Christ's coming by great preachers such as C. H. Spurgeon, G. Campbell Morgan, C. E. Macartney, Alexander MacLaren, and others.

ISBN 0-8254-4051-3   **160 pp.**   **paperback**

Classic Sermons on the Sovereignty of God **Warren W. Wiersbe**
Sovereignty. All authority, power, dominion, and majesty belong to God. Warren W. Wiersbe has chosen twelve classic sermons that capture the glory and grace of this divine attribute. Included are sermons by Paul Little, R.A. Torrey, C.H. Spurgeon, and Jonathon Edwards. Excellent "starter" material for sermon preparation; solid spiritual content for devotional readers.

0-8254-4055-6   **160 pp.**   **paperback**

Classic Sermons on Spiritual Warfare **Warren W. Wiersbe**
In a timely new compilation of classic sermons, Dr. Warren Wiersbe offers eleven expositions dealing with various facets of Satanic activity. Included are sermons by such outstanding preachers as William Culbertson, Allan Redpath, D. Martyn Lloyd-Jones, G. Campbell Morgan, C. H. Spurgeon, and others.

ISBN 0-8254-4049-1   **160 pp.**   **paperback**

Classic Sermons on Suffering **Warren W. Wiersbe**
Sermons by such illustrious preachers as C.H. Spurgeon, Phillips Brooks, John Calvin, Walter A. Maier, George W. Truett, and others that will uplift the depressed, comfort the heartbroken, and be especially useful for the preacher in his pulpit and counseling ministries.

ISBN 0-8254-4027-0   **204 pp.**   **paperback**

Classic Sermons on Worship **Warren W. Wiersbe**
In these classic sermons by pulpiteers such as C.H. Spurgeon, John A. Broadus, James S. Stewart, Frederick W. Robertson, G. Campbell Morgan, and Andrew A. Bonar, we discover the true meaning of worship and are challenged to practice it.

ISBN 0-8254-4037-8   **160 pp.**   **paperback**